"...And Then The Music Stopped Playing"

Ken Ward

Braiswick at By Design
Felixstowe, Suffolk
01394 273200

ISBN 978-1-898030-11-9

Printed by Lightning Source
Braiswick is an imprint of Catherine Aldous Design Ltd

Acknowledgements

To Joyce, without whose patience and help as computer 'techie' and Assistant Editor, this book could never have been produced.

To my children Stephen, Adam and Carla, who read through the manuscript, making constructive suggestions.

To Jackie Short, Bruce, and all the members of the Ladygate Scribblers, who encouraged me and patiently listened and read through some of my chapters.

To John Blackman, Rod and Tina Scott, Andrew Auster of Orwell Park School, Anthony Parker, Ian Paterson, Desert Rat web site, Bovington Tank Museum and Alec Marsland who all supplied superb photographs.

To The Institute für Stadtgeschichte Frankfurt am Main who supplied the pictures of Frankfurt, The Jüdische Museum Frankfurt an Main, Archiv, A157 who supplied the picture of Ablaufplan der Deportationen von der Großmarkthalle aus, and Günther Rath for his photograph of the play ground and rear entrance of the Wöhlerschule.

To Waltraud Giesen and Feli Gürsching, who helped with valuable information and the picture of the Wöhlerschule playground.

Contents

Dedicated to the memory of my parents and brother who were murdered in the holocaust and to all my friends and comrades who were killed fighting the Nazis with me so that future generations will be free.

They gave their lives.

Their memory is immortal to us.

Siegfried, Trude and Hans

Prologue

"I am speaking to you from No. 10 Downing Street. This morning the British Ambassador in Berlin handed the German Government a final note, stating that, unless the British Government heard from them by 11 o'clock that they were prepared at once to withdraw their troops from Poland, a state of war would exist between us. I have to tell you now that no such undertaking has been received and that consequently this country is at war with Germany..."

For a few moments the hushed silence continued. So it was war, my father had been right. Then pandemonium broke out when everybody started talking. Within minutes the air raid sirens started a penetrating up and down wailing but we were told not to worry, as it was only a test alarm.

On the 3rd September 1939 I sat on a chair in the large hall, which served as a dining room in the hostel in Margate-Cliftonville, clutching the square cardboard box firmly to my chest, as it contained my gas mask. I had only been evacuated here yesterday from London with 5 other boys. Some 60 children sat in a circle round a table, on which stood a wireless.

I had only arrived in England 9 days earlier, on the 25th August, as a Jewish Refugee from Germany with a group of children. For nine days I had experienced an unknown freedom. I was not suppressed any more.

I was suddenly an equal. I could walk down the road freely without being afraid that I might be beaten up by a group of Hitler Youth.

My English was still poor, but I had understood every word of Neville Chamberlain's speech. We were at war with Germany. We were at war. My parents were still there. How could I now help them to get out of Germany? How could I communicate with them?

In spite of being in a hostel with other refugee boys, I felt very alone. But my mother would find a way. Somehow or other she would manage to write to me and make contact. She knew I was safe in England; I would have to be patient and wait.

How long would the war last? At my age of only 16 years, would it last long enough for me to be old enough to join the army and help to fight and defeat the Nazis? Would I, as a German refugee, be allowed to join the British army? Of course I was not to know that the war was going to last for 2,175 days and that fifty to fifty-five million people were to die.

The Happy Child

Mama walked into the kitchen, where the nurse was drinking a cup of coffee and asked her, "Have you changed the dressings of the baby?"

"No, he is sleeping so peacefully so I do not want to disturb him."

"Hell," mother replied, "The doctor gave us strict instructions to change the dressings every three hours. You better come with me and we have a look at the boy."

Mother fumed and hurried into the master bedroom, followed by the nurse and noticed that there was blood dripping out of his cot. They had to rush a doctor to the bedside to stop the haemorrhage caused by the religious ceremony, in which it is customary for Jewish boys to be circumcised when they are 7 days old. Had mother not hurried into the bedroom and called for the doctor very quickly, then that is where my life story would have ended.

Seven days earlier, the 29th November 1922, had been a miserable, rainy day. I was born at 5.30 in the afternoon as my mother did not like to have her sleep disturbed. The birth took place at home, in Frankfurt Main, Germany, in our third floor flat. I was the fourth son.

My father Siegfried Würzburger (Papa) was 45 years old and practically blind. He had been born with his retina damaged. One of the skeletons in the family cupboard was the rumour that Amalie,

Würzburger boys 1925
from left to right Hans, Walter, Paul and Bubie

my grandmother (Omama), had tried to abort the birth, thus causing the damage to his eyes.

My mother Gertrude (Mama) was 33 years old and already had three boys. My eldest brother Hans was 11 years old, Walter was 8 and Paul 4. I was named Karl Robert but as I was the youngest I was called Bubie, which is a common practice in Germany, and just means 'little boy'.

My father and mother were Liberal Jews, although my mother had come from an orthodox family. The Jewish community in Frankfurt was reasonably large, and the Liberal section had its own synagogue, where my father had been employed as the organist since its inception in 1911. He also had his own private music school and was teaching piano, organ, singing and musical theory, and composing occasionally.

I grew up within a very happy and close-knit family unit. Our third floor flat consisted of seven rooms, one of which was the music study, in which my father gave lessons.

One of my first memories is sitting under the grand piano, looking at its three wooden legs, the pedal hanging down in the centre front, and the brass frame with the strings above me. Outside this field of vision, I could only see my father's legs working the pedals, and the legs of the pupils standing near the piano. They were practising Schumann and Schubert songs, operatic arias and, when several pupils gathered together, they sang duets, trios, quartets etc. I was allowed to sit and listen under the grand, whilst keeping very quiet. The moment I started moving about, or making noises, I was gently ejected by the scruff of my neck, like a little kitten.

Our flat was opposite a huge private estate, which was surrounded by thick walls mounted with broken glass. Opposite the road widened and in the centre was a large island on which stood the Hessen memorial, an old war memorial. It was surrounded with a large area of hard-pressed sand,

Hessen Denkmal Betmann Museum on right
Ken's birthplace one of the buildings on the left

Hessendenkmal, ca. 1910   S7A 1998/37.110
© Institut für Stadtgeschichte Frankfurt a.M.

3

where, when I was about four years old, I was allowed to play with friends.

We also played in the nearby Anlage, a strip of parkland surrounding the whole of northern Frankfurt like a horseshoe, with each end touching the river Main. This strip of parkland had been planted where the old town walls used to be. There were special playing areas for children with sand pits and tennis courts and music bandstands with little cafés, where concerts were frequently given. Newspaper stalls also sold sweets, where I always pestered Mama or Omama to buy me something.

As we were a very close family I usually played with my brother Paul as he was only four years older. When Hans and Walter reached the age of thirteen they were each given a bicycle, and both of them had a saddle fitted for me on the crossbar, so that they could take me along for a ride. Walter often took me to an open-air swimming pool on the river Nidda, a tributary to the river Main.

There was a doorbell on the front door and letterboxes in the entrance hall for all the different flats. We had a buzzer inside our flat to let people in and I would watch them come up the stairs. We still had gaslight on the staircase but already had electric light in the flat. There was no central heating so we had large tiled stoves in each room, which had to be lit in the winter and the fires were kept going round the clock. A fire also had to be lit in the boiler in the bathroom, whenever we had our weekly bath.

There were no fridges or freezers at that time, but there was a metal-lined cool box kept cool by placing large cubes of ice into it, which were delivered about three times a week by a horse-drawn van. A large basket hung at the back of the van which contained large chippings of ice. In the summer I ran after the van with my friends and when the driver was on his front seat, where he could not see us, we pinched ice chippings from the box sucking them with great delight.

In the dining room, where we had our joint family meals, there was a piano on which Mama gave piano lessons. In addition she gave English and French lessons. She was also a part-time teacher at an elementary school.

Papa's lessons were very hectic. When giving lessons to a gifted pupil, and there were many of them, he completely lost all track of time, well over-running the lessons, which often meant we had to wait for him before eating. One of his most quoted remarks to Mama was, "We can have dinner in five minutes, but I'll just give a one-hour lesson first."

Papa's initials S.W also stood for 'South Wind', as he used to stand a lot with both feet firmly planted on the ground, the bottom part of his body steady as a rock and the top part of his body moving constantly from left to right, his eyes tightly shut. He adopted this stance when he was thinking deeply or when he was discussing interesting subjects.

We had a live-in maid from the country called Annie. The girls changed over the years, but they were still always called Annie. Annie did the cooking and cleaning and looked after Paul and me. We must have been quite a lively and noisy family, because the landlord, who lived in the flat below, came up on numerous occasions, always with the same opening remark, "Oy Herr Würzburger, my ceiling is coming down," in his very broad Frankfurt dialect.

The synagogue where my father played the organ was about four kilometres from our flat. We went to the synagogue every Friday evening and Saturday morning and on all the religious holidays. Orthodox Jews are not allowed to travel using a vehicle on the Sabbath, as it is a day of rest. Liberal Jews tended to use either cars or public transport. Cars were parked a little distance at the back of the synagogue so that other members of the congregation did not see them.

As we did not have a car we had to go by tram. There was a direct line from our home to the synagogue. On some occasions my father was late, particularly on a Friday evening, after having given a '5 minute' one-hour lesson, lasting one and a half hours. He would then rush to the tram stop, accompanied by either my mother or me, and wait impatiently for the tram to arrive. As soon as he got on the tram he would give the driver and conductor 50 Pfennigs (half a Mark) each, asking the conductor to ring the bell at each stop as quickly as possible so that the driver could start and drive as fast as he could.

Shortly before my 4th birthday, in November 1926, Mama took me to a toyshop and asked me to sit on a tricycle to see if it was the right size and make sure I could reach the pedals. I was so disappointed when she did not buy it. About a week later, lying in bed waiting to go to sleep, staring up at the ceiling, I spotted a brown paper parcel on top of the wardrobe, with tiny red wheels sticking out of the wrapping. I felt certain that it was the little red tricycle from the shop. The two days to my birthday were an eternity.

The day of my birthday arrived at last, but I had to wait for the long-established family ceremony to be carried out before I received any presents. The family formed up in line in the hall, in front of the closed dining room door. Father in the lead, followed by Mama, and all the boys in order of age. The birthday boy was then asked to go to the front and slowly lead the column into the dining room, whilst we all sang the family song to a tune composed by my father many years ago. The lyrics went, 'Beat the drums and wave the flags, hey children we shall have such fun, when we march to the birthday table today, march, march, march!'

The door opened, there it was, the red tricycle, standing in the centre of the birthday table with some other toys, chocolates and sweets. I could not wait to get on it and rode round and round the dining room table all day long.

***

My aunt Recha, my mother's sister, had remained very orthodox. She had four daughters called Gustel, Ruth, Margot and Edith. The four girls were all a year apart in age, except for Ruth and Margot, who were two years apart. I just fitted in between the gap. Because they were so close in age to me, I often played with them.

In 1926, when I was about 4 or 5 years old, their father Max bought a car, which at that time looked huge to me. We went on family outings in this car, with us children sitting on little stools between the flap-down seats fitted to the partition and the deep rear seats. My uncle often had to struggle to get the car started with the starting handle. We drove to the Taunus, a mountain range not far from Frankfurt with the highest mountain, the Feldberg, being about 2,700 feet high for picnics in its deep forest.

On Sundays we often went for day excursions, taking the tram to the base of the mountain range, going for long rambles through the mountains. As a special treat we sometimes had a meal at one of the many restaurants, either halfway up, or on top of the Feldberg. We leisurely walked along the easier routes, mainly because of my father's blindness. Mama linked arms with Papa, reading a book to him, either a thriller or German translations of English authors, Joseph Conrad, Mark Twain and the Swedish author Knut Hamsun. I used to listen in, run ahead and hide behind trees, lie down under a tree, gazing up through the gently moving branches into the sky, watching the clouds skimming over the mountain tops. Even at that young age the shapes of the clouds fascinated me, seeing animal shapes and human faces in them. I believed the faces I could see were people who had just died and were floating up to heaven to become angels.

There were wild strawberries, raspberries and blackberries to pick and eat on the spot.

During 1928 and 1929, there were many political demonstrations in the streets of Frankfurt by both the Communist and the Nazi party, and whenever the two met, there were fights and shots were often

Recha Scharlack (aunt) with daughters Gustel,
Ruth, Margot and Edith

exchanged, people were injured and sometimes even killed.

When there was such a political demonstration we children were not allowed out of the house, but watched from the safety of our third floor window as one or other group marched past the Hessen memorial. Sometimes there was a torchlight procession with a band marching in front, the Nazis singing wartime marching songs and the Communists singing 'The International' and Russian marching songs. After one of these processions passed our house we heard shots as they reached the Anlage, the nearby strip of parkland. Soon afterwards we heard the siren of police cars and an ambulance.

***

On New Year's Eve we always gave a party. Perhaps the most memorable was in 1928. The

Bubie aged 5yrs

students helped to decorate the flat and built little cubicles with different designs, representing different countries and different cultures. One student made a huge dog out of paper maché with large glowing red eyes, which flashed on and off. The beast was much taller than me and I kept my distance when I was allowed to get up at quarter to twelve, to see the New Year in, and take part in some of the merriment. I was allowed to watch the dancing to the live band and the games being played by the adults. Fireworks were let off in the streets outside and in the park opposite, similar to the displays in England on Guy Fawkes Day.

The atmosphere was always joyous and happy. Drink and food were in abundance. Mama said to me, "Bubie, come and have some French bread with my green butter." She had made quite a reputation with her green butter, which I had watched her prepare many times. Hard-boiled eggs

House Party in Frankfurt 1926/27 Music students and family
Siegfried sitting 2nd row on right Trude last row on far right
Max Scharlack 1st row 3rd from left
Recha Scharlack 2nd row left in sleeveless black dress

chopped very finely and mashed into butter with chopped chives, parsley and other herbs. I just loved to eat it.

Standing about were small hand-carved black wooden elephants with long trunks, and rhinos with their pointed horns sticking out, displaying pretzels on the trunks and horns.

"OK Bubie, you are only allowed one pretzel from one elephant and one rhino," I was clearly instructed. I loved them so much, that I swore to myself that when I grew up, I would have my own elephant and keep it fully supplied with pretzels, so that I could eat as many as I liked.

These parties must have been very avant-garde for the inter-war years. There were no racial or religious differences. Everybody was equal according to his ability.

Some ten years later, when I was 16 years old, Mama took me into her confidence saying, "You know those lovely parties we held at New Year with our pupils, before Hitler came to power?"

"I well remember them and only wished I had been older, so that I would have been allowed to stay up and take part, like Walter, who played his saxophone and clarinet in the band."

"Well," she continued meekly, looking at me somewhat embarrassed, "Perhaps things were a bit too easy going. You know your cousin Inge, who lives in London now and who you will meet there again when you go to England? She became pregnant with Charlotte at one of our parties and had to marry her cousin Ludwig, who was not the father, in a bit of a hurry. She never told us who the actual father was."

I was now learning about the skeletons in the family cupboard.

***

One day when I was about 6 years old, I said to my friend Fried, "Come on, let us play postman."

"Good idea," said Fried, "but as postmen we will need letters which we have to deliver, where can we get them from?"

I had a brainwave. All the houses in our street had letterboxes for the tenants in the doorways outside the front doors of the block of flats. I slid my small hand easily into the slot on top of one of them and was able to pull out a few letters. We walked half way round the block, each collecting a large amount of letters, which we tied into bundles like we had seen postmen carry. We then walked

12

round the block in the opposite direction delivering the letters into other letterboxes which all bore the names of their owners. This was great fun. As neither Fried nor I had started school, we could not read and the letters were just dropped into boxes at random. When we grew tired of playing postman, we both still had an abundance of letters left which I took home quite happily.

Mama saw me come in with the letters under my arm, "Bubie, what are those letters you have there?"

"Oh, I have been playing postman with Fried."

"Yes, but where did you get all these letters from?"

"We got them out of letterboxes along the road and then we posted some into other boxes."

I did not even see the hand coming that gave a stinging slap to the side of my face. Mama said, "No use you crying, you know you can't take letters out of other peoples post-boxes, that is stealing."

Now I really started crying.

"You just stop crying," said Mama. "We now have to put the matter right. All these letters you have got here belong to somebody. Their names and addresses are on the envelopes. You will now come with me and we will put the letters into the boxes where they belong. I will show you where each letter has to be delivered. Unfortunately we won't be able to do anything about the letters you have posted in the wrong boxes, but can only hope that the recipients will take them to their correct addresses."

Needless to say, I never played postman again.

My hair at that time was cut pageboy fashion nearly reaching to my shoulders. At Easter 1929 I was aged 6 years and 5 months, old enough to start at school. My hair had to come off and had to be cut to a proper boys haircut. Mama took me to the Gents Hairdresser next door to our house and asked him to give me a short back and sides.

The barber said, "I have been waiting to do this for a long time. After all, Karl Robert has to look like a boy."

And to his great delight my beautiful long hair fell to the ground.

It was customary at that time in Germany for children to be given a large sugar bag on their first day at school, so that they would not cry when left at the school by their mother. This Zuckertüte was a huge cone shaped bag of coloured paper, filled with sweets and chocolate. Sometimes it was nearly the size of the child. I had always badly wanted one of these bags and was looking forward to getting mine. However, Mama decided that this would be bad for my teeth, but relented by giving me some sweets and chocolates when I came home from my first day at school.

The Schwarzburg Schule was an elementary school about a 20-minute walk from home. After I had been taken there several times I was allowed to walk there by myself. On the first day on my own I was very concerned whether I would find it, running all the way with my small satchel, that was carried on my back and contained a Griffelkasten, a box containing slate pencils, ordinary pencils and crayons and a square slate in a wooden frame, too large to fit into my satchel so being tied to it and hanging at the back, swinging precariously with every step I took. When I finally arrived I was greatly relieved to see the school was where it was supposed to be.

School started at 8 am finishing at one o'clock. Here I had my first introduction to reading and writing. It was a boys school and there was a girls school next door, with a fence separating the two playgrounds. Even though we were only six years old discipline was very rigid and teaching very formal. Right from the early stages we were given homework and had to practise writing letters, initially with slate pencils on slate board, gradually progressing to writing on paper, first with pencils and crayons and then with real ink. We felt quite grown up when we were given ink in the inkwells of our desks and started using pens.

The schooling system in Germany at that time meant you were compelled to attend elementary school until reaching the age of ten. If your school reports were good enough, and if your parents were willing to pay a small fee, which at that time was about 20 Marks per month, you attended grammar school for a period of nine years and then go on to university if you had passed your A levels, or leave after six years having obtained the equivalent of the O-level examinations. If your school report was not good enough, you had the choice of continuing at the elementary school for another four years and then take on an apprenticeship or go to a middle school for six years.

I found life reasonably easy at the elementary school. I was able to keep up with the pace and was always amongst the top of the class without really having to make much effort. This proved to become a great disadvantage when I joined the grammar school at the age of ten, because I suddenly found that I had to make much more of an effort to keep up with the class.

Some of the fathers of boys in my form were Nazis and their sons were also supporters of the Nazi party. They were the only children I did not play with. They were somewhat isolated, because the majority of the class held them in contempt.

***

In 1931 we moved from our flat opposite the Hessen memorial to a flat on the fourth floor of a block on a corner near the beautiful Frankfurter Opera House. We could see it from our dining room window overlooking the front, with the chestnut trees reaching up to the fourth floor and lining the main road, the Bockenheimer Land Strasse. Directly opposite was a huge private park contained within a wall. In the centre stood a mansion occupied by one of the members of Rothchild family.

One of the many reasons for moving to the new flat was that it was much more central and nearer the synagogue where Papa played the organ. The rent was also cheaper. There was a large hall with a table and chairs, a bookcase on one side and bookshelves and bookcases lining the long wall to the dining room on the right. The dining room, apart from the large dining table, settee and sideboard also had a piano, on which my mother gave piano lessons. There was an alcove with more bookshelves, a little table and a serving hatch to the large kitchen. The dining room was at the corner of the building and had three windows, which were all full of plants.

The main music room where my father gave lessons was to the left front of the flat. It was very large. It contained two grand pianos, a Steinway and a Blüthner. It also had a radio and gramophone with four speakers, one in each corner of the room. There were two large bookcases along one wall containing volumes of music; several scores of all the operas, to enable music students when participating in ensemble lessons to sing the various parts of a quartet or trio. There was a desk with a typewriter, which I was allowed to use at times, and a comfortable settee with a large brass-smoking table in front. Next to the music room, extending to the back of the building, was also a very large bedroom with two big beds pushed together, forming a wide double bed for my parents, with a large wardrobe next to them. At the foot end was a single bed for me. There was a wide passage next to me, and the wall was lined with two wardrobes. On the wall by the window was a hand washbasin with an electric water heater. There was a wide door into the music room, which was always shut, and next to it stood a big chest of drawers and on it were two hand washbasins with carafes of water standing in each. Next to that was my toy cabinet and a tall wind up, upright HMV gramophone, which had been discarded by my father and been given to me. On the bedside cabinet next to my fathers bed was his tall tin of bicarbonate of soda, which he had to take frequently for his indigestion, and his pocket watch, which was the family time piece used by us all.

At weekends, I often crawled into the centre of my parent's double bed, lying contentedly between them, cuddling them both and I loved being cuddled by them. I was very proud that they often called me their 'reconciliation child'. I only knew it was something nice because they always said it very lovingly but did not know what it meant.

One day, when I was alone with Mama, she said to me, "Bubie, do you know why we sometimes call you our reconciliation child?" When I shook my head she continued, "At Christmas 1921, Papa had bought me a ticket for a four-week cruise on a luxury liner, starting in January from Hamburg, going round Spain, via Gibraltar, through the Mediterranean to Italy, Greece and then to Egypt. It was a fantastic holiday for me to travel on this liner, to be waited on hand and foot, and to spend a day in each of the many ports we called in, on both the outward and return journey via the North African coast. I made friends with many people on board, and we are still friends now with Hans and Martha Fuchs.

I noticed that Papa was behaving a little bit strange when I arrived back home, and after I had been back for only a few days, I asked him what was wrong. He confessed that he had been having an affair with a young, very pretty pupil of his, who was very talented and who had a beautiful soprano voice. Of course I was very upset and slept on the settee in the dining room for a week. Papa too was very distraught, assured me that the affair was finished, asked me to forgive him, and I decided to move back into our bedroom."

I was quite taken back when she finished and said,"Who is the pupil Papa had the affair with?"

"Oh, Bubie, you don't know her, I made sure that Marlene would never come to music lessons again. Anyway, we made up, made love, you are the result, and that is why we call you 'our reconciliation child'." When she then took the opportunity to explain to me the facts of life, I listened open-eyed and in wonderment and was very proud to be a love child. I wondered how many more skeletons would come out of the family cupboard.

My eldest brother Hans used the room between the music room and the dining room. In addition we had three attic rooms on the floor above us, one was used by my grandmother Amalie, and the others by Walter and Paul.

A windowless passage with hangers for coats on the wall led to a separate toilet next to the bathroom, which had a wood fired boiler.

I remained at the same school until Easter 1933, but of course had to travel much further now. I went by tram, interchanging in the centre of the town onto another tram. The fare at that time was 10 Pfennigs in each direction. I still remember a great altercation soon after we moved. I decided to walk home from school and of course arrived an hour late. I had spent half of the fares on sweets and proudly presented my mother with the 5 Pfennigs I had saved. However, this was not appreciated the way I expected it as my mother had phoned the school to find out if I had been given detention when I had not arrived on time.

***

On the opposite corner of the house where we lived was a café, which was also a bakery. They had a special counter where they sold home-baked cream cakes and gateaux, ice cream and chocolates. There was a smart, comfortably furnished dining room with tables and chairs, where coffee and cakes were served. All the daily newspapers were on display, chessboards were available and customers played chess, spending hours playing, reading and drinking coffee and having snacks.

We were on very friendly terms with the owner and when Papa gave an evening concert at home, with the music students performing, we borrowed their chairs.

My grandmother Amalie, my father's mother, helped in the household and looked after all the cooking and shopping. She allowed me to help and taught me how to cook and bake cakes. My mother was very busy teaching piano, English and French to private students at home in addition to teaching part time languages and religion at a local school.

My brother Paul one day said, "Come on Bubie, let us play cowboys and Indians."

I happily agreed.

"You are going to be the Indian. Stand over there by the wash stand," he said. "Come on, stand up straight and I will catch you in my lasso and take you prisoner."

Paul then swirled the rope menacingly over his head, letting the rope fly straight towards me. I ducked. The rope flew over me, Paul tugged on it. There was an almighty crash as both the bowl and a full water jug smashed to smithereens on the floor. After the initial shock and silence that followed the door next to me flew open and Mama dashed in, took in at a glance that I was standing on the sodden floor amongst the smashed bowl and jug. I never got the chance to duck to avoid the hard blow aimed at my cheek.

✳✳✳

I liked to play records on the tall wind-up gramophone I had been given by Papa. One of the records was the final aria of Cavalleria Rusticana, sung beautifully by Caruso. The label read 'Mama Adios' and it was, of course, sung in Italian. The music is very sad and compelling, and I imagined in my mind that Turidu, the son, had joined a cavalry regiment, was singing his very sad farewell song to his mother, as he knew that he was going to be killed in battle and that he died soon after finishing his song, when right at the end a woman's voice shouted *Turidu est morte*. I played this record incessantly, with tears streaming down my face. Only when I was much older did I get to know the lyrics of this opera properly and eventually sang the aria myself, when I had singing lessons from Papa.

When going to sleep at night I could always hear my father's pupils play the piano or singing arias or when several pupils came together for an ensemble lesson, singing duets and quartets. I went to sleep listening to Schubert songs and most of the Italian operas, to Wagner and Offenbach, and later sang many of these myself. From the age of ten I was allowed to go to the opera house, just across the road by myself and my parents bought me the tickets.

One of the first operas I saw was Hänsel and Gretel and Der Freischütz, both of them making great impressions on me, with the children lost in the deep forest and caught and imprisoned by the wicked witch in the first one and the man selling his soul to the devil for a magic bullet to win a prize at the rifleman's festival in the second one. I shall never forget the deep valley, with thunder and lightning, when he met up with the devil.

I watched La Boheme, Il Pagliaci and Cavalleria Rusticana, Traviata, Tosca and the Meistersingers. I came home after hearing Helge Roswenge, a fantastic tenor, singing his aria in Flotow's Martha, and having clapped so loud with the audience that he repeated it twice, excitedly telling my father about it. He stopped his pupil, who was just putting on his coat, and got him to sing the aria "Martha, Martha Du entschwandest, und mit Dir mein ganzes Glück...." (Martha, Martha you have disappeared, and with you all my happiness) just for me. I have loved listening to opera ever since.

I loved my singing lessons, but found piano lessons difficult, especially as everyone else played brilliantly. Of course I did not practise enough and Papa insisted that I spend at least one hour a day playing the piano. When it was my turn to have a lesson I was asked, "Bubie, did you practise one hour each day since the last lesson?"

When I replied, "Sorry Papa, but I was so busy with homework, I did not manage to get all the hours in," the usual reply was, "As a punishment you will not get a lesson today."

I then immediately rushed off on my bike to a swimming pool, relaxing in the sun and enjoying my free time. That's why I never learned to play the piano, regretting it now, but I have never lost the need to listen to beautifully played music.

***

In 1932 our house was being re-decorated on the outside, scaffolding had been erected round the house, reaching from the road to the roof. Planks were on the scaffolding on each floor, with ladders going up from each level.

One day our only toilet was locked for ages, several people needed to go there urgently, and when my mother knocked on the door, there was no response. Nobody appeared to be missing. In desperation Mama broke the door lock to get in and found an empty toilet, with the window wide open. It was soon discovered that the culprit had been my brother Walter, who had climbed out of the toilet window and re-entered the flat through the bedroom window.

***

At that time there was a lot of talk about Hitler and the Nazi party. The Weimar Republic was very unstable, with constant changes, unemployment had risen to 3½ million, and Hitler promised work for them all. Gangs of Brown Shirts, with their swastika armbands (SA) were marching up and down the streets waving flags and shouting anti-Jewish slogans.

Siegfried Würzburger
playing his
grand piano
1936

The general opinion was that Hitler would never be able to win an election. Papa was not so certain, "He might just be able to get in, and if you get vermin like that coming to power, you can never be certain what is going to happen. Anyway Bubie, you keep away from all demonstrations and don't play with children whose fathers are Nazis."

I did not need that sort of advice, only a few of the boys in the fourth year of my elementary school were Nazis. They were the rougher element and I had no intention of making friends with them.

I was not concerned with politics. My best friend Heinz Jochen Stiege and all my other friends, none of them Jewish, always played together. We were a very happy crowd, worked quite hard at school, because at the end of the fourth year, at Easter 1933, it would be decided, based on how well we had done, whether we would stay on at the elementary school or go to a grammar school.

We talked sometimes about what we wanted to be when we were grown up and I said to Heinz Jochen, "I want to go to a Grammar school when we have finished here I want to become a doctor, perhaps a surgeon."

He replied, "Oh yes. I too want to go to grammar school. I want to follow in the footsteps of my father, who is a director of a very large industrial organisation."

Our decisions were made and we lived and played on contentedly, until this peaceful equilibrium of mine was suddenly shattered, when Hitler came to power on the 30th January 1933.

I had arrived at the school as usual. After about an hour a teacher came in and whispered something to Mr. Ebel, our class teacher.

After he left, Mr. Ebel called me over to his desk and said, "Würzburger. I want you to go home right now, don't play about, but go straight home. It is for your own safety. Your parents will explain."

That's how the first happy ten years of my life ended.

The Second Class Citizen

Papa and Mama, of course, were very upset about the rise to power of Hitler. Mama believed he would not last very long.

In the last term at the Musterschule, a local grammar school, my brother Walter had participated in producing a very modern end-of-term play, 'Der Weg zum Glück' (The Road to Happiness) at the Schauspielhaus, the main theatre in Frankfurt. It was performed with great success at the end of 1932 and I was allowed to go to the performance. At the end of the play, when the curtain fell, the lights did not come on and I wondered what was happening, getting ready to leave, when Walter stepped in front of the curtain and said, "What are you all still doing here, why don't you go home?"

Another chap came on and said, "They are waiting for the 'Happy End', and so far it was not very happy. Was it?"

"Ah, well, that is different, we have got to make it a 'Happy End'. Come on raise up the curtain."

Up went the curtain, the whole cast came out onto stage, Walter started playing his saxophone, the other students joined in with clarinets, saxophones and trumpets, and the youngest, there were about fifty pupils in the first and second school years, only ten or eleven years old, playing on toy saxophones, which they hummed with great gusto. Then Walter came to the front of the stage,

"Well this is better, this is a 'Happy End', so now you can all go home."

He bowed; the curtain came down to loud applause. The lights came on and we went home.

Walter, who had just started university, was by now very accomplished on the saxophone and clarinet and loved playing jazz music, which my father abhorred. Walter decided he would have to leave Germany immediately and I still remember the deep concern of my parents when he said, "1 can't stay here in Germany. The Nazis are persecuting all Socialists, Communists and Jews. They are taking away all our freedom. I am going to Paris with my clarinet and saxophone and will try and get a job in a dance band. If it comes to the worst I will just have to become a street musician."

No sooner was that said and he was off. At the beginning of 1933 it was still quite easy to leave Germany and he had no problems getting into France. However, he needed a labour permit to play in bands. Sometimes he managed to get a labour permit, some bands even engaged him without a permit, and there were times he had to play in the streets to earn a crust.

Things started to change very fast in Germany. On the 28th February 1933, only one month after Hitler came to power, Papa rushed into the room after having listened to the news on the radio and said, "They have burned down the Reichstag in Berlin, a Dutchman Marinus van der Lubbe has been arrested."

There was stunned silence, the Reichstag was the parliament building. Parliament could not meet. Papa said on the following day, "President Hindenburg has signed an emergency decree, giving Hitler dictatorial powers. Socialist and Communist delegates and Trade Union Leaders have been arrested in the early hours of the morning by the Nazis and have disappeared. There will be no more free democratic parliament in this country. The Nazi dictatorship is beginning."

When I travelled on the tram to school that morning people were still openly discussing the Reichstag fire. One man said, "Well, they have arrested a Dutch Communist and are accusing him of having started the fire. 1 would not be surprised, if he is just a fall guy and the fire was actually started by Goering. The fire is just too convenient for the Nazis to get rid of all opposition in parliament and sort out the Communists."

Within a few weeks open political discussions could not be held in public.

At first things went on as usual at my elementary school, which I was to leave by Easter. Gradually some of my friends befriended the boys who were Nazis, and who had been previously shunned by us. I suddenly realised that I had fewer friends.

Easter approached, the time when the new term started in German schools so my parents saw Mr. Ebel, my form teacher, who told them that I had done very well at school and suggested that I should go to a grammar school.

Papa and Mama said, "Well Bubie, this is a very good school report. We want you to go to a grammar school. It will cost us DM20.00 per month

(Approx. £2.00), but we still want you to go, and expect you to work very hard."

Papa added, "I don't want you to go to a Jewish school. I want you to go to the Wöhler Gymnasium, a Christian school, which is walking distance from our house, as the discipline will be much better. All your brothers went to the Muster Schule, also an excellent Christian grammar school, but it is too far for you to travel. Anyway, the Wöhler Gymnasium is a modern grammar school. This means that they teach French and German as modern languages and concentrate on sciences, not like some of the older schools that still teach Greek and Latin."

So the decision was taken and I was eagerly waiting for the last week of term to come.

A lot happened during that period. There were continuous marches of the SA (the Brown Shirts) carrying burning torches at night, led by bands mainly beating the drums or brass bands with standard bearers carrying huge swastika flags. They were always singing military marching songs, anti-communist and anti-Jewish songs. The refrain of one line was 'When the Jewish blood runs from our knives'. These SA marchers, in their brown shirts with epaulettes, leather shoulder straps, wide belts with large metal buckle and daggers attached in leather holsters, marching noisily in their brown leather knee boots, were very frightening to me. They were soon joined by H.J. (Hitler Youth) and BDM (The girls in the Hitler Youth) on marches, always led by a band of drummers with very long slim drums, waving their sticks high up in the air and producing a very monotonous boom, boom, boom, in time with the marching.

Very soon all political parties, apart from the National Socialist Party (The Nazis) had been banned, including even the Boy Scouts and Girl Guides. Members of these youth organisations were compulsorily transferred into the H.J. and BDM.

Swastika flags were hoisted on all public buildings. The square surrounding the opera house had swastikas flying every few yards around the edge of the square.

It became compulsory for all men to become members of the N.S.D.A.P. (National Socialist Workers Party), and most of my school friends joined the Hitler Youth.

The last week of term arrived and I went with Mama and Papa for an interview at the Wöhler Gymnasium where I met some of my old classmates, including my best friend Heinz Jochen Stiege. We saw Dr. Hirsch our form teacher and a photograph was taken of the new intake. We both were allocated into the Sexta A (first year grammar school) and told what schoolbooks to buy for the start of term and were shown around the school.

I said to Heinz Jochen, "Gosh, this is a huge school, I don't know if I will ever find my way around it. Look at that immense school hall with its big stage, on which the school orchestra had just been playing. And what about that big lab, with all its bottles and test tubes."

He replied, "Don't worry, we will soon get used to it, but don't buy any textbooks yet, because I heard that the pupils who finish the first year will

*Frankfurt
1933-45
under the
Nazis*

be here on the first day to sell their textbooks to us,
the new intake. I have been warned that when
buying a secondhand book from a previous pupil,
you must make sure that he has not torn any pages
out and that the book is reasonably clean."

That was good advice given at the right time.

I enjoyed the Easter holidays, went swimming a
lot, not knowing I would not be able to do that
much longer, as eventually Jews were not allowed
to use public swimming pools. When term started
two weeks after Easter, I reported to the school and
Dr. Ritter told us, "I am your new form teacher. Dr
Hirsch is not here any more, he has gone to teach at
a Jewish school."

As we settled down at the wooden desks with a lift-up lid and storage place inside and an open inkwell on the right hand side, into which we dipped the nibs of our pens. Dr. Ritter handed out a revised list of school textbooks. Some of the history books had been replaced with new books, produced very quickly by the State Education Office controlled by the Nazis, proclaiming the superior Aryan and Germanic heritage of Germany.

Propaganda against Jews and Communists quickly became very strong. Dr. Goebbels, who had become Minister of Propaganda, made violent anti-Jewish speeches to vast crowds who cheered loudly and chanted, 'Juda Verrecke' (Death to the Jews).

Wöhlerschule Grammar School in Frankfurt
School entrance photo Easter 1933
Ken 1st row 4th from right

One of the gutter-press papers, vehemently anti-Jewish, Der Stürmer, became more and more popular. It specialised in articles denigrating Jews, inventing stories of good true German Aryans being exploited by Jews, of rape and violence by old Jewish bearded men of innocent German Aryan virgins, spoiling the German race. They re-hashed old gory stories of Jews killing Aryan babies and using their blood for cooking unleavened bread for Passover. The front pages depicted grasping old bearded Jews with huge hooked noses robbing their innocent German victims.

The Aryan race in contrast was shown to be tall, clean, blonde and blue-eyed. They were strong and sportsmanlike, shown doing physical exercises, or marching in columns with spades or rifles over their shoulders, giving a strong military image. My school friends who had joined the Hitler Youth wore smart uniforms, shirts with epaulettes, short trousers with wide leather belts and a metal buckle with the swastika engraved on it. They started to go to camp, where they marched with specially designed rucksacks called an Affen (Monkey), with a blanket folded squarely around it and mess tins dangling from the back.

The curriculum at school was changed to fall in line with this dogma. History books disappeared from the shelves and were replaced with new editions. Hitler's book *Mein Kampf* became the German bible and every school boy was proud to possess a copy. More and more shops started displaying notices 'Jews are not wanted in this shop'. Jewish stores were boycotted with Storm Troopers standing outside the stores, who had painted big slogans on the windows, 'Germans, defend yourself, do not buy from Jews'. Any member of the public daring to go into the store faced the prospect of being badly beaten up. With all this propaganda, I too started to believe that I was inferior, kept well out of the way of groups of Hitler Youth standing about on the pavement in order to avoid any problems.

More and more books were banned, not only books by Jewish authors. Papa called me in and told me on the 1st May 1933, "1 have just listened to the radio, you will stay indoors today. They have just announced that students, led by their professors, together with Storm Troopers, were burning banned books in a huge bonfire outside the Berlin State Opera House. This will be followed by other bonfires burning books, in all the major towns, including Frankfurt. I do not know exactly where they are burning the books in Frankfurt, so you stay indoors and keep well out of the way." With tears in his eyes he added, "You know, they are burning Thomas and Heinrich Mann, you know how I like these two authors. They are also burning Sigmund Freud, Karl Marx, the children's book by Erich Kästner 'Emile and the Detectives' and Erich Maria Remarque's 'All Quiet on the Western Front', you have read both of them."

On the next day Papa told me, "There is more bad news, Dr. Siegel, a Jewish lawyer I know in Munich had gone to the police asking for protection against the SA terror squads. They handed him over to the storm troopers, who are now police auxiliaries. They shaved off his beard, cut off his trousers and marched him through the town carrying a placard which read 'I shall never again complain to the police'. I have also heard that Himmler is supposed to have established a concentration camp at Dachau, where they are sending all Communist, Socialist and Trade Union Officials."

Hitler was broadcasting continuously in 1933 and a Volksempfänger (Peoples Radio) was sold cheaply by the thousands, to enable the people to listen to the Führer. The general greeting in the streets, in shops and at school was now 'Heil Hitler' with a smart lifting up of the right arm.

One day, when we had assembly in the school playground, the swastika flag was hoisted and we had to stand to attention, with the right arm raised, and sing the two German National Anthems, 'Deutschland, Deutschland über alles' (Germany, Germany above everything) and the Nazi 'Horst Wessel Song' (composed by a Nazi close to the Führer, a marching song) 'Raise the flag high, march along in closed ranks, comrades let us shoot the Communists...' The songs were long, my arm ached and I tried to support my arm surreptitiously with my left arm.

A classmate standing next to me pushed me slightly and said, "You are not allowed to support your arm. You have got to be tough like us and not weak like the Jews."

I had to participate and had no option but to sing out loud, with my arm raised high until the end of the songs, and lower it then with great relief.

I came into the classroom one morning as one of my friends was drawing a Stürmer type of sketch of a Jew, bent over, with a hooked nose dribbling,

The burning of books in Frankfurt

onto the blackboard. Another boy who had seen me come in, nudged my friend, who turned round, blushed and wiped off the offensive drawing on the board.

On the whole I was treated quite well and was tolerated more than befriended. However, we still played games together. One of the boys, Carl, said to me in the school playground during the break, "Come on Würzburger, let's drop water bombs onto the teachers."

No sooner said than done. We ran up the main staircase to the third floor, filled two paper bags each with water and looked precariously out of the centre window above the main entrance. We saw two junior teachers approach the entrance.

Carl said, "Würzburger, we drop the bags just as they get on the first step leading up to the entrance door. That's it, let go now and run."

The four water bombs accelerated in speed towards their unsuspecting victims. We did not stop to watch, but ran down the back staircase and mingled with all the other boys in the school playground. We soon found out that we had hit our

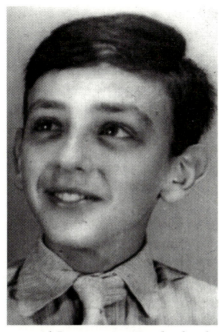

*Bubie as a
15 year old boy*

target and I got a pat on the back from one of the boys.

I was quite musical and music was my best subject. I was in the choir and in 1934 we produced the 9th Symphony of Beethoven at a school concert. In spite of being Jewish, I was allowed to sing in the choir with my strong soprano voice and my parents were allowed to come to the performance.

In June 1934 1 was travelling in the tram when a heated discussion took place.

One man said, "They shot Röhm last night, the leader of the SA."

Another replied, "It was the Führer himself. He shot him because he was a homosexual. He found him in bed with a member of the Hitler Youth."

"No," said another one, "that wasn't the reason, Hitler has known that for a long time Röhm was getting too big for his boots, he wanted to take over from the Führer, so Hitler had to eliminate him personally."

"But most of us have been members of the SA for a long time," said a fourth man, with a big swastika badge stuck in his lapel, "I have been a member since 1927. Röhm was my leader, he was always a close friend of the Führer and always stood by his side. I can't believe that Hitler shot Röhm. It must have been Himmler or one of his men. The SS have always been very jealous of us SA and wanted to take over from us. I bet this is the first step to get rid of our SA."

I listened with open ears to the discussion. Shortly after Hitler came to power public discussions no longer took place. If anyone made

Alte Wöhlerschule
School playground
and back entrance

an anti-Nazi comment he was very quickly arrested and not seen again for quite a long time. This open discussion, with many participants, was unheard of by June 1934. Certainly, shortly after the killing of Röhm and 200 of his supporters, which became known as the night of the long knives, no more such discussions were allowed to take place.

As all my friends were in the Hitler Youth, going on sports exercises and rambles at weekends and to youth camps, I wanted to do something like that myself. I joined a Jewish Zionist boys group in 1933, the Habonim, and we went on rambles together in the mountains of the Taunus and the public forests surrounding Frankfurt. Sometimes we ran into larger groups of Hitler Youth and were then duly beaten up, unless we could first beat a quick retreat. We got quite good at that, by keeping a good look out, which was the responsibility of the leading member and the last one walking in the group. We had weekly meetings. Our leader was called Uri, a boy aged about 16 or 17. We read books about Palestine and greatly admired the first Jewish settlers, who carried arms to defend themselves and who were continuously harassed and attacked by Arabs.

One day Uri said, "We really ought to have a uniform, as we are a legitimate youth organisation. We already have dark grey shorts and we ought to have blue shirts with epaulettes. Does anyone know somebody who could make these shirts at a reasonable price?"

"Oh yes." I said, "My uncle Max is a cloth wholesaler and he can also get garments made, I can find out from him whether he is willing to help us and how much it will cost. What colour blue did you have in mind Uri?"

"I think a light blue would be best, like the colour of the shirts the Jewish settlers wear in Palestine."

"Right," I replied, "I will see what I can do to get a shirt each, for the twelve of us, and report back to you at the next meeting."

I went to see uncle Max the next day, he told me that he was very busy, but that he could make us twelve long-sleeved shirts with epaulettes and an outside pocket on the left breast at a reasonable price, out of a job lot of cloth in the right colour blue, which he had been left with. He needed to know the chest measurement of each boy and the length of sleeves required. He told me to take the measurement on the outside of the arm from the beginning of the shoulder to the wrist and on the inside from under the arm to the wrist. He told me again that he was busy, and would fit this work in, but could not promise a quick delivery, but it should not take longer than four weeks.

Armed with all this information, I happily went to the next meeting and within a week got all the measurements from the other boys. The shirts duly arrived four weeks later, and were a great success. I wore mine with great pride. Subsequently we all ordered an additional short-sleeved shirt.

In the summer of 1934 I went with the Habonim to a youth camp at Wildhaus in Switzerland for two weeks. It was a revelation to come out of Germany, to see the last swastika flags on the shores of Lake Constance, as we crossed into

Switzerland, to be in a country where you could speak freely and where you did not see swastikas hanging about from every window and flag pole. The camp was on a hillside, which solved the toilet problems as latrines had been built going down the slope, with a ditch running from a water tap at the top, through the latrines, into a cesspool at the bottom. All you had to do, when you had used the toilet, was to turn on the water tap at the top. We were in circular tents holding fourteen boys, and slept in sleeping bags wrapped in a blanket and a ground sheet. Unfortunately it rained non-stop for eleven days out of the fourteen days we spent there. We all had sore throats and there was a camp doctor visiting the site daily.

We all got the same instruction. "Gargle, come back tomorrow." He soon got the name of 'Dr. Gargle'.

We went for long walks through the mountains, had campfires at which we sang German folk songs and Jewish songs, jumped through the high flames when the campfire was really blazing well, put on plays mimicking and making mock of Hitler. We felt great. We did not know then, that we would never be able to do that again.

One day, at one of our meetings Uri told us, "It is very important that you always obey your parents and do whatever they ask of you. However, if you want to do something you care about very much and they object then you must go ahead and do it just the same, whatever the consequences. Because if you obey, and give up on everything that is of no great importance to you, they will give in and let you do what you want to do."

41

It is a lesson I always remembered, I found it worked and I carried on with this philosophy for the rest of my life, both in the army and at work.

I shall never forget coming back from that holiday and suddenly being in an atmosphere of restriction and fear. Most of my fathers many pupils were of course non-Jews and they all said, that the fact that he was Jewish would not make the slightest difference to them.

They kept on saying, "You are the best music teacher in Frankfurt, I won't go anywhere else. Hitler does not mean you when he condemns the Jews. You are a good Jew, you are a German, and your father and grand fathers were German. He only refers to the bad Jews, the Poles who have come here to exploit the good German Aryans for so many years, who give the Jews a bad name and of course the rich Jews, that have been living off the fat of the land without doing anything."

But in spite of their assurances, very slowly, pupils stopped coming to lessons.

I was again very excited, as it was my twelfth birthday. I was awake very early, waiting for the rest of the family to get up, so that we could all march together to view the birthday table, which had been prepared the previous night in the dining room, as was the family tradition. The door opened, and there were the presents from all the members of the family lying on the table and my first secondhand grown-up bicycle was leaning against it.

I opened all the other presents excitedly and gave everyone a cuddle for giving me such nice presents. But the best was the bike, and Papa and Mama got a special thank you.

Paul said, "It's not fair and right that Bubie should get a bicycle on his twelfth birthday. All of us boys only got our bikes for our Barmitzvah, when we were thirteen. We were always told we can't have bikes before that, because we are too young."

Mama replied, "That is right Paul but things are different now, we do not know what will happen in the future with Hitler in power. It is important that Bubie too should be mobile like all of you. Why don't you go down into the street with Bubie, pick a quiet section in the side street and teach Bubie on his birthday how to ride a grown up bike."

"Yes, come on Paul, please help me and show me, the bike is very big and I can reach the pedals when I am sitting in the saddle, but can hardly touch the floor."

Paul relented and got quite excited at the prospect of teaching me how to ride a grown-up bike, as previously I had only had a small bike, which I was allowed to ride on the pavements. I very carefully carried my new bike down the stairs from the third floor, Paul got his bike out of the cellar and we pushed the two bikes along the road into a side street.

Paul said, "Right, Bubie, you will have to do exactly as I tell you. You have to be very careful. Now first of all, push the bike right next to the curb and sit up on it, facing in the direction you want to go."

I did as he asked and could only just touch the edge of the pavement with my toes.

"To start you off, I will push you whilst you pedal," said Paul, "when I let go, carry on pedalling and I will catch you up on my bike."

This is what we did, I peddled and wobbled a lot and after only a short distance I came off. By that time Paul had caught up with me and we continued the exercise many times, with Paul being very patient, giving me tips on how to peddle and keep my balance better. I soon became sufficiently proficient to be allowed to go out by myself.

The winter in 1934 was very cold and the river Main froze over solidly. The snow was cleared from the ice so that people could go skating on the river. I went as well, dressed very warm in a heavy coat and a balaclava type of helmet, knitted by my grandmother. I am not a good skater and kept falling over. Everybody enjoyed skating on the river Main and there was no hostility towards me, perhaps they did not notice that I was only a Jew.

The same happened the following February at the annual local carnival. It went on for two or three days. Everybody dressed up in fancy dress and walked and danced along the streets. Most adults had a lot to drink. There were booths with food and drink, sweets and chocolate to buy. I dressed up as a Red Indian, with headgear made by Mama. She had also made the jacket I was wearing. My face was painted dark brown and I could mingle with the crowd with no one suspecting me of being Jewish.

Now it was early summer. I am on my own in the Brentano public swimming pool on the river Nidda. I have ridden here on my bike, which I have parked safely in the bike shed. I am lying on the grass, in the warm sun by the rivers edge. The water is rippling gently at the side, flowing towards the river Main. I am dangling my hand in the water. It is so peaceful. There are only two swastika flags flying over the entrance gate. Fortunately there is nothing else to remind me, that I am just an unwanted inferior being. I can relax. I am saying a silent prayer, 'Please God, make Hitler see that he is wrong about the Jews. If he knew Papa and Mama, our family and friends, he would know that we are good people and not grasping Jews, who are trying to exploit the Germans. Please make him see this and stop persecuting us.'

Having said my prayer it was time to go for a swim. I got up and looked into my bag for my blow-up ring, which I always used, as I was only learning to swim. I had left it at home. I was not prepared to miss my swim just because I had forgotten my ring. There was nothing for it but to go into the pool and have a try without it. I climbed down the ladder into the deep end of the pool, where I had always been swimming with my safety ring. Once in up to my neck, I started swimming along the edge of the pool, always ready to grab the handrail at the side. Lo and behold, I could swim; I could keep my head above water. It was only a breaststroke, doggy fashion, but I swam.

I cycled home as fast as I could, carried the bike down the cellar steps to its allocated place and ran up the three flights of stairs, taking two steps at a time, ringing the doorbell several times impatiently.

Mama opened the door and said, "What is the matter Bubie, what is the rush?"

I blurted out excitedly, "Mama, Mama, I can swim, I went to the Brentano bath without my blow-up ring and I can swim without it."

"Oh that is great news, well done. Papa will be so pleased because it will be so much nicer for both of you when you go swimming with him at Moslers in the river Main. Actually he had only told me this morning that he wants to go swimming with you tomorrow."

I never took my ring to a swimming pool again.

When I came home from school the following day Papa said to me, "Come on Bubie, let's go to Moslers".

I guided Papa across the road to the tram stop, being his eyes, as usual. We got off at the river Main and walked on to the squared off wooden structure, that jutted out into the river. On the wooden gangway alongside the riverbank were the changing booths. In each booth were coat hangers and a small door at the back. You placed your clothing on the coat hanger, knocked on the door and an attendant would open it, take your clothing and give you a numbered tag. We then walked along the wooden gangways enclosing the swimming section of the river and I guided Papa to the steps leading into the water. We swam about to our hearts content in the river Main, which then was quite clean and not polluted, and I had to guide Papa again to the ladder leading out of the pool.

On the way home Papa said, "We will go to the little restaurant at the back of the Kettenhofweg.

They have got an excellent kitchen, they know us there and we are still welcome."

When we arrived there the owner came over to greet us, "Hello, Herr Würzburger, come in, nice to see you. So you have got Bubie here with you today. He is growing up fast. We have got some very nice calves liver today, quite fresh and we serve it with our special potato salad. I know you will enjoy it."

We did enjoy an excellent meal, and I felt very grown up. During the meal Papa told me that Hitler had passed the Nuremberg laws forbidding Jews to be in certain professions, freezing bank accounts, making them second class citizens and making sex between Jews and non-Jews a capital offence. I was really too young to understand all the implications at that time.

A few days later there were great celebrations in Germany, as the Saarland was returned to Germany after a League of Nations Referendum. The Nazis claimed full credit for this and we schoolboys were chanting jubilantly, "Deutsch ist die Saar, Deutsch immerdar." (The Saar is German and will be German forever).

On the 8th July 1936 my parents were informed by the school, that I was not welcome there any more as a pupil, as the school wanted to be Judenrein (clear of Jews) and that they should send me to a Jewish school. On leaving I was given my school leaving report, and to all our surprise, the Headmaster of the school, Director Dr. Jung, a fervent Nazi, wrote in his own handwriting under remarks, 'Würzburger is leaving our school to join the Philanthropin. We discharge him with our best wishes for his future.'

When I arrived at my new school, the Philanthropin, I was greeted by the director Dr. Driesen with, "Ah, Würzburger, here comes the last of the Mohicans, welcome to our school." He explained to me that I had been the last Jewish pupil in a non-Jewish state school in Frankfurt, and introduced me to my new class and the form teacher Dr. Weil.

I soon realised that the discipline was very lax compared with that of the Wöhlerschule but felt more comfortable in these surroundings. I made new friends and went out swimming and cycling with them. In the summer the class went on a school outing to the Felsenmeer in the Odenwald, but it was becoming more and more difficult for Jews to go on these outings.

I left the school after the Kristallnacht in 1938, when the Nazis burned down the synagogues, in order to learn a trade before emigrating from Germany. As I liked cooking very much, and had helped at home with cooking and baking cakes, I was sent to the boarding house of Frau Schild, to be trained both in the hotel trade and as a chef.

When I had finished my course I had the opportunity during the summer of 1939 of going to an agricultural training camp at Rütnitz near Berlin, to be trained for possible emigration to Palestine. At the bottom end of the fields was a railway line, and at night we could see long goods trains slowly rumbling by, with German soldiers

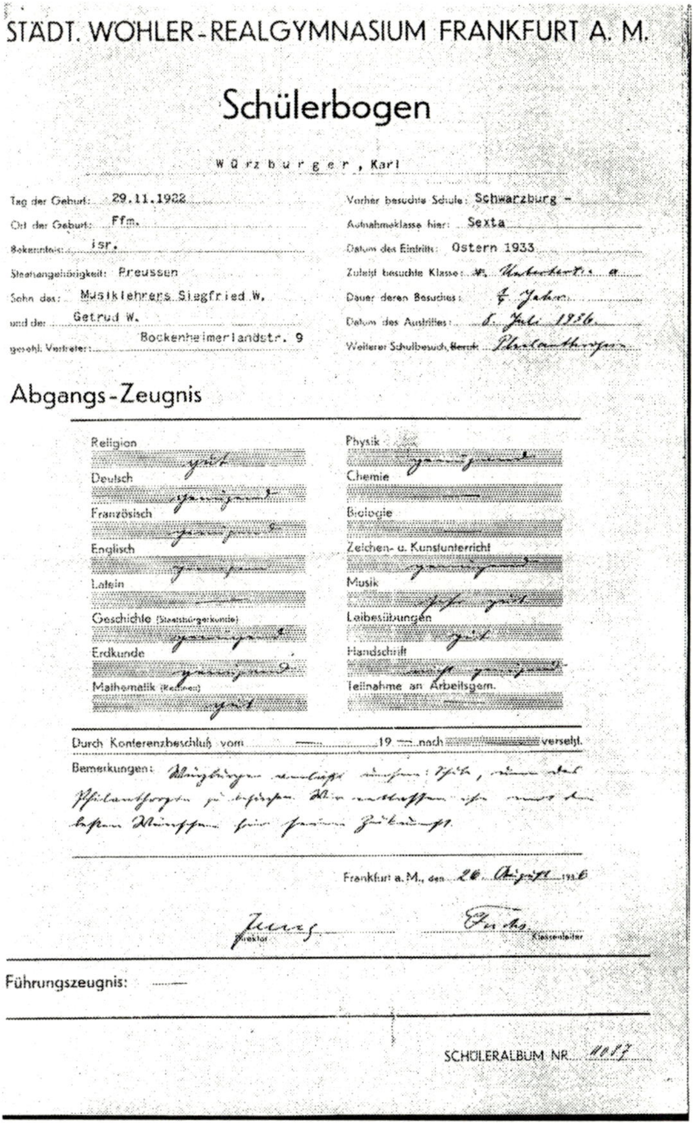

STÄDT. WÖHLER-REALGYMNASIUM FRANKFURT A. M.

Schülerbogen

W ü r z b u r g e r , Karl

Tag der Geburt:	29.11.1922	Vorher besuchte Schule:	Schwarzburg -
Ort der Geburt:	Ffm.	Aufnahmeklasse hier:	Sexta
Bekenntnis:	isr.	Datum des Eintritts:	Ostern 1933
Staatsangehörigkeit:	Preussen	Zuletzt besuchte Klasse:	Untertertia a
Sohn des:	Musiklehrers Siegfried W.	Dauer deren Besuches:	¾ Jahr
und der:	Getrud W.	Datum des Austrittes:	6. Juli 1936.
gesetzl. Vertreter:	Bockenheimerlandstr. 9	Weiterer Schulbesuch, ~~Beruf~~:	Philanthropin

Abgangs-Zeugnis

Religion	gut	Physik	genügend
Deutsch	genügend	Chemie	—
Französisch	genügend	Biologie	—
Englisch	genügend	Zeichen- u. Kunstunterricht	genügend
Latein	—	Musik	sehr gut
Geschichte (Staatsbürgerkunde)	genügend	Leibesübungen	gut
Erdkunde	genügend	Handschrift	nicht genügend
Mathematik (Rechnen)	gut	Teilnahme an Arbeitsgem.	

Durch Konferenzbeschluß vom —— 19 — nach versetzt.

Bemerkungen: Würzburger verläßt unsere Schule, um das Philanthropin zu besuchen. Wir entlassen ihn mit den besten Wünschen für seine Zukunft.

Frankfurt a.M., den 20. August 1936

Direktor Klassenleiter

Führungszeugnis: ——

SCHÜLERALBUM NR. 1037

Wöhlerschule leaving report

sitting in cattle trucks. We knew then that it would not be long before the Nazis would attack Poland.

**

One night I had a terrible dream. I dreamt that I woke up in the middle of the night and heard street singers and musicians outside our bedroom window. I went to the window, lent out and saw them three floors below on the pavement opposite, with a beautiful woman lying on a robe. I leant out to see them better, lost my balance and fell screaming out of the window. As I hit the ground I woke up in bed in a sweat with my heart pounding. It took me a long time to get to sleep again.

This dream kept repeating in exact detail for many weeks and I was very frightened, until one night I woke up and heard the same singing again. I was drawn to get up and go to the window and knew that if I went to the window I would fall out.

Ken Odenwald Philantropin Jewish School outing May 1938
Ken is in front row 2nd right

So I held on to my bed and forced myself to stay in bed. I was in a cold sweat and very frightened. As I stared at the ceiling and the window, holding on for dear life, I realised the music was slowly disappearing and then it had gone. I was wide-awake now, and stayed awake for a long time and I never had the dream again. But after that I was always very cautious when looking out of the bedroom window.

A street singer accompanied by an accordionist had sung arias from operas on the pavement opposite our bedroom window in the previous year. He had an excellent powerful tenor voice. My father heard him, gave me some coins to wrap in paper to throw out to him, and asked me to call down to him, requesting him to come up. When he came up, we found out that his name was Albert. Papa explained to him that he was a singing teacher and that Albert was very gifted, that he was prepared to give him free singing lessons and started immediately to give him a lesson, in spite of the fact that the next pupil had just arrived, who was made to sit in on the lesson and just wait.

Albert came to have a few lessons, but he loved travelling and only stayed in Frankfurt for a short time. Whenever he passed through Frankfurt, he first sang a few arias on the pavement opposite and then came up to see us, to fit in a quick lesson. Papa begged him not to waste his beautiful voice but to become a singer at the opera, but Albert wanted to be free as a bird and travel about and earn his living as a street singer. I think we last saw him at the end of 1935 or the beginning of 1936. We believe that eventually he was arrested as a vagabond and sent to a concentration camp by the Nazis who classified Romanies and Vagabonds as sub-human. It is most unlikely that he survived, as I found out after the war that 200,000 to 500,000 Gypsies were murdered in the holocaust.

Frankfurt Central Railway Station

Goodbye Bubie

The final decision for me to leave Germany on my own was made after I had left home quietly on the afternoon of the 10th November 1938, aged 15 and had stood aghast in front of our Synagogue, which had been burned down during the Kristallnacht. My father, who was blind, had been the organist and his beautiful organ had been destroyed. The Catholic caretaker who had tried to prevent the Nazis from entering the building had been knifed and was critically ill in hospital. There were only two options. To emigrate to Palestine or go by Kindertransport to England.

On 24th August 1939, at 7.30 in the morning, I was leaning out of the window of the train at the main station in Frankfurt, with an address label hanging round my neck. The platform was empty apart from a few policemen and three SS men strutting about importantly in their black uniforms and black jackboots. Only Mama had been allowed to bring me to the station but she was not allowed on the platform. I saw her standing lonely and forlorn by the main pillar to the station roof at the barrier. Even from this distance I could see that she was crying. Tears welled up in my eyes, but I tried to control them, after all I was the oldest child in the compartment holding eight children, some of them crying, holding Teddy Bears, and the youngest not even understanding why they were on the train without their Mummy or Daddy. There were three

JÜDISCHE WOHLFAHRTSPFLEGE

FRANKFURT AM MAIN   RÖDERBERGWEG 29

Abt. KINDERTRANSPORTE

Herrn/~~Frau~~

Augzbürger

Betr. ENGLAND-TRANSPORT AM ...**24.8.39**...............

Wir teilen Ihnen hierdurch mit, dass Ihr.. Kind/Kinder.......
..**Karl**... unter Permit-Nr..**0418** zu dem nächsten England-
Transport am ...**24.8.**............... eingeteilt ist/sind.
Es wird der Zug 7.57 Uhr ab Frankfurt a.M., benutzt. Treff-
punkt ist 7.15 Uhr am Blumenstand in der Haupthalle des Frankfurter Hauptbahnhofes. Das Handgepäck ist dort zusammenzustel-
len, es wird in unserem Auftrage von einem Gepäckträger in das
Coupé befördert. Jedes Kind muss einen Pass, bezw. Kinderaus-
weis mit sich führen. Für das Passagiergut sind 2 Listen anzu-
fertigen, die von der zuständigen Devisenstelle abzustempeln
sind. Die Listen müssen mit folgendem Text überschrieben wer-
den: " FÜR TEILNEHMER AN DEM KINDERTRANSPORT DER JÜD. WOHL-
FAHRTSPFLEGE, FRANKFURT AM MAIN AM .**24.8.**...... NACH ENGLAND."

In der Anlage übersenden wir Ihnen ~~eine Bescheinigung zur Vor-
lage bei den Behörden~~ und eine Anweisung der Transportleitung.

Das Gepäck muss 1 Tag vor Abgang des Transportes zollfertig
gemacht und aufgegeben worden. Die hierzu nötige.. Fahrkarte..
ist/sind am.....**22.8.39.**...... bei uns entgegen zu nehmen.

Jedes Gepäckstück sowohl Handgepäck als Passagiergut ist mit
einem Anhänger der Reichsbahn zu versehen. Auf der Rückseite
des Anhängers ist in BLOCKSCHRIFT und mit Rotstift der Name
und die Permit-Nummer des Kindes zu schreiben.

                              Hochachtungsvoll

                              JÜDISCHE WOHLFAHRTSPFLEGE
                              FRANKFURT AM MAIN
                              Abt. Kindertransporte

*Letter authorising Kindertransport for Ken's departure from
Frankfurt on 24 th August 1939*

coach loads of children aged 3 to 16, with only two adults accompanying us.

On the day before my last day at home, my father said to me, "Come on Bubie, sing for me your favourite aria from Tosca."

He played the opening bars on the grand piano and I sang it in my tenor voice, the way I had never sung it before, rising effortlessly to the high C. As I turned to look at Papa for approval, I saw that tears were streaming down his face. I had never seen him cry before. I rushed and embraced him to comfort him, only realising then that the lyrics of the last line I had sung in German, were, "My hour is passing and I must die despairing. How cruel is death. Life was never sweeter."

I hugged him tight and said, "Papa, it is only a song, please don't cry. I am only going to England. I will be all right there and safe from the Nazis. As soon as I get there, I will do everything I can for you and Mama to come to England as well. Anyway, as soon as the Nazis have gone, I will come back."

Papa said, " Yes, I know, how silly of me, but whatever you do, when you get to England, try and continue with your singing and voice training."

I leant out even further to see Mama for the last time, as the steam engine started puffing away noisily and pulled the train gently out of the station with a last hoot. I comforted some of the crying children, we started playing games and the crying soon stopped. We were all afraid of going to a new country, whose language we did not speak, not knowing where we would be staying, who would be looking after us. At the same time I was very excited about getting out of Germany, not having

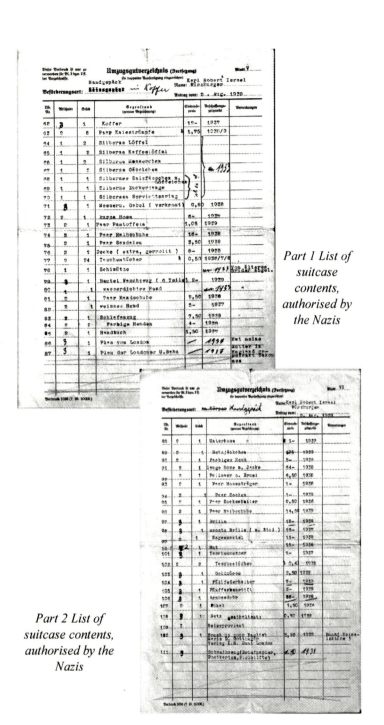

Part 1 List of suitcase contents, authorised by the Nazis

Part 2 List of suitcase contents, authorised by the Nazis

56

to be afraid any more of walking down the streets, avoiding groups of Hitler Youth, who would set about me and beat me up.

We settled down on our journey, ate our sandwiches and I became very apprehensive as we approached the Dutch border. The train came to a sudden halt at a German station and SS guards in their black uniforms joined the train.

One entered our compartment, checked our papers and picked on my suitcase demanding that it be opened. He searched through my neatly and tightly packed case, emptied it onto the seat, looked at some of the items and then said I could pack it up again, leaving me struggling to get everything back into the case.

I looked out of the window and saw a girl of about 15 who had been taken off the train with her

Hans, Trude and Siegfried Würzburger August 1939
on balcony of Frankfurt flat

luggage, her address label swinging round her neck, being marched into an office, as the train started moving off again.

We crossed the Dutch border and pulled into a station. The doors had been locked so that we could not leave the train but we opened the windows and talked to the crowd of Dutch people who were standing on the platforms and who knew that we were in a Kindertransport (childrens transport) escaping from Nazi Germany and going to England. They were very kind and friendly, asking many questions about Germany, giving us drinks of hot chocolate and biscuits.

The train went on to Hook van Holland, where we boarded the night ferry. In the morning I went on deck and saw ahead of me the English coast with its high white cliffs. Now I felt as free as the seagulls noisily flying round the ferry as we docked. I could not wait to land; soon we were on an English train, where I could not understand the conductor properly, although I had learned English at school for a year.

The Refugee

We arrived at Liverpool Street station on the 25th August 39, exactly nine days before the outbreak of the Second World War. Members of a Jewish committee, who called out our names from lists they carried, met the whole group of children.

One woman shouted, "Where is Karl Robert Würzburger."

I jumped forward and she took my luggage and me to a waiting taxi, which drove us to my great excitement through London to 9 Brondesbury Road in Kilburn. Mrs. Hyams looked after six refugee boys like myself in a basement flat. The others who had been there for several months, showed me round Kilburn, walked with me to Marble Arch. A new world had opened up for me, where I was an equal, could walk about freely and eat white bread with butter, an unknown delicacy.

Life was so different from Germany. There was a friendly bustling atmosphere in London. The newspaper vendors shouted out the latest news headlines. When they wanted a tea break, they just left the stalls with all the papers on it. If you bought a paper, there was a tin on the box into which you placed your money and took your change. I loved London.

As it looked as though a war was imminent, we were issued with gas masks. On the 31st August all six of us were evacuated to a Refugee hostel in Margate Cliftonville. I immediately wrote to my parents and gave them my new address. The hostel, an old boarding house, was very cramped. There were 3 or 4 children to each room. The food was good but sparse, so we were hungry most of the time. We had fourpence pocket money per week. For threepence we could go to the cinema, at a special price for refugees. We walked along the sea front and I bought a pound of broken biscuits for a penny from Woolworths to supplement our food. When I was made head boy I was paid an extra shilling for my work and responsibility. This made life much easier for me.

I listened to Neville Chamberlain declaring war on Germany at 11 am on the 3rd September 1939. Aged sixteen I was one of the oldest boys in the hostel. People were very friendly to us, in spite of the fact that we were Germans and that there was now a war on. I was occasionally invited to homes for tea, which was a special treat. By speaking to English people and reading children's books my English improved rapidly.

I could now only communicate with my parents via friends in Holland, who forwarded my mail to them. On the 20th October was Mama's 50th birthday, and I managed to get a special birthday letter off to her in time.

Shortly after that, the hostel father told me, "Würzburger you have to report to the Margate Town Hall at 3 p.m. to have your status checked. Take all your papers with you."

I only had a German children's identity card with my name, German address, date of birth and a great red "J" stamped across it.

I arrived at the town hall on time and was ushered into a huge chamber in which twelve good citizens sat round a horseshoe-shaped table, where I was told to sit on a chair in the centre of the horseshoe, facing the investigators. Although I was sixteen years old, I only looked about fourteen and felt very frightened and intimidated. They tried to put me at my ease, asking if I spoke English? When did you arrive in England? Where are your parents? Do you like it here? And then came the killer question, Do you want us to send you back to Germany?

I just cried out, "Please don't send me back, I only just arrived here, if you send me back, although I am a German and was born in Germany, the Nazis hate all Jews and they will just kill me. Since I have been in England, I have been able to walk about for the first time without being afraid."

There was silence, the chairman spoke quietly to the others and then told me, "You have nothing to be afraid of, but report to Margate police station tomorrow morning."

When calling at the police station I was promptly issued with an Alien Registration Book and classified as a 'Friendly Enemy Alien'. This meant that I would not be interned, and my only restrictions would be to register with the police whereever I lived, that I would not be allowed out in the streets between midnight and 6 am, and that I would need a permit if I wanted a bicycle and if I wanted to work.

At the end of the month I was sent to a hostel in Finchley Road, London. I decided, that as I was now 17 it was time for me to find a job and stand on my own two feet and save the Jewish Committee, who were looking after me, money. Easier said than done. As a 'Friendly Enemy Alien' I had to get a labour permit to work. There was still a lot of unemployment and many boys in my age group were looking for work. Being a foreigner, the labour exchange could not offer me any jobs, but suggested to find my own and then apply for a labour permit.

I started looking for jobs at hotels and boarding houses as a trainee houseboy, with a chance to train as a cook, as I had gone through a cookery-training course in Germany before emigrating. I found a number of very good jobs, went to the labour exchange with them, who then offered them for a week to English boys, who gladly took on the good jobs I had found.

Eventually I managed to find myself a job as a houseboy in a boarding house near Swiss Cottage in Hampstead, which no English boy wanted as a lot of the guests were foreigners and the houseboy had to be able to speak German.

I had been promised an interview with the owner of the boarding house, who was also a Jewish refugee from Germany but had lived in England since 1934. I arrived at Swiss Cottage tube station well on time. I walked to 11 Adamson Road and stared up at the imposing building with its massive stone steps leading up to the entrance door high above. I walked up to the front door in trepidation, fearing I would be turned down. However, I was lucky and was offered a job to be trained in the hotel business. I was to work 87 hours a week with only every Saturday afternoon and every second Sunday afternoon off, after 3 pm. As part of my salary I was given a small room on the second floor and all my meals. Washing and ironing my clothing had to be done in my rather limited free time.

I started work at 7am scrubbing the massive front steps and worked alternately until 8pm or 10pm cleaning rooms, serving at tables, helping in the kitchen and being a general factotum, all for the princely sum of seven shillings and six pence per week (37.5 pence in our present currency). This was not as little as it appears, as for sixpence of the old money I could buy myself ten Woodbine cigarettes or go to the cheapest seat in the local cinema.

Mrs Rankin, the cook, had a flat in the basement and invited me often down after work, and we sat round her fireplace with a roaring coal fire, something I had never seen before, sipping tea and chatting away happily.

I took great delight in riding on the running boards of the London taxis, when I had to hail one from the corner of Finchley Road for our guests, always hoping for a tip.

One of my many duties was to ensure that all the blackout curtains were drawn at night and that there was no light showing or the Air-raid warden would come along and shout the dreaded words, "Put that bloody light out."

The Blitz

On the 10th July 1940 the Battle of Britain started. One night my boss, Mrs Bendheim, knocked frantically on my door.

"Come on Charlie, (a substitute for Karl) come down to the basement quickly, there is an air raid on."

I rushed down and was frightened all night by the Luftwaffe planes droning overhead, the whistling of bombs dropping down and the anti-aircraft guns firing incessantly. In the early hours we could see the London docks burning fiercely in the distance.

About three weeks later a local pub was damaged and the Embassy Theatre at Swiss Cottage was hit during the night. We all joined in to clear away the rubble and salvaged the chairs.

One night Chris, one of the maids, suggested we go down to Swiss Cottage tube station and sleep down there on the platform. There were double metal bunks with wire mesh, and she hoped we could grab an empty one.

There was a tremendous community spirit on the platform. People brought down blankets and pillows, shared food and drink. Some played musical instruments and we sang songs. The tube trains kept running until late at night and their rumble kept us awake, but we could not hear the bombs dropping.

When we emerged from the station in the morning I said to Chris, "This is all very well, but nothing has happened here last night, I think I would rather stay in the house, take my chances, so that I can see what is going on."

It was now time for me to change jobs in order to get away from the 87-hour week, but I needed to find somewhere else to live first. I found some digs in the same house in Kilburn where I first stayed when I had arrived in England. Mrs Hyams, the landlady now rented out several rooms to refugee boys, giving us full board, which included sandwiches to take to work. I had to share a room with only one other boy and paid one pound per week.

I had managed to find a job as a trainee Eastman cutter in a factory producing war uniforms in Osnaburgh Street, near Great Portland Street Station. I now only had to work 48 hours a week and my starting wage was one pound and ten shillings. A workman's return ticket from Kilburn to Great Portland Street station was sixpence per day, two shillings and sixpence per week.

On the third day at work, old Mr Ravden, the boss, who was a Polish Jew, chatted to me and said, "Do you live at home with your parents?"

"No, I live on my own in digs in Kilburn. My parents were unable to leave Germany as my father is blind and could not get a visa to emigrate to any country. I managed to get here on my own with a Kindertransport, just before the war broke out. I have to pay one pound a week and that includes full board. But I am much better off now than in my previous job where I worked for 87 hours on domestic duties. Now I am learning a very interesting new trade and I would really like to become a tailor."

The governor replied, "Well, if you put your mind to it we will train you but first you will have to learn to become a cutter."

He never said any more but with my first pay slip I was paid one pound fifteen shillings and two weeks later he upped it to two pounds.

The London tube trains and buses were terribly crowded. Everybody was very friendly, people were chatting to each other and telling everybody what had been happening in last night's air raid.

I had to queue up everywhere. Air raids started early, searchlights lit up the sky, anti-aircraft guns were firing during the air raids. Petrol was rationed but those people who had cars stopped at the bus stops offering lifts, shouting out of their windows where they were going. In spite of my accent whenever I was asked where I came from I was treated politely as an equal.

There were now raids every night and I was listening to the large forces of German Dornier bombers droning overhead. It was an unmistakable sound, very frightening as they approached. You could hear the whistle of the bombs dropping ever closer, I buried my face under the pillow, counted the bombs dropping, breathing out with relief when the last bomb had come down.

Now that I was financially better off I had saved up enough money after a few weeks to buy myself a secondhand bicycle for four pounds. Having obtained permission from the police to use it I started cycling to work.

A government inspector came each week to check the uniforms and had to stamp them before we were allowed to pack and dispatch. One day the inspector refused to pass the battledress trousers, because the colours did not match on the seam.

Sam, one of the bosses, came over to me and showed me the rejected trousers and said, "Look what you have done."

I blushed and realised, same as Sam had, what had happened. I had to lay up lengths of cloth on a very long cutting table and the several layers were made up of different bales of cloth, which varied in shade. When cutting out the trousers and then bundling them up for the machinist, you match each pair up by taking the layers from the top. I had inadvertently turned some stacks of trousers over, causing a mismatch when bundling up.

Sam felt sorry for me and said, "Don't worry, I will see to it."

The following evening, just before closing time another inspector, who was a friend of Sam, arrived and stamped all the faulty trousers with his WD stamp. We packed them and shipped them out.

We took it in turns at night to be on fire watch, on top of our six-storey factory building. One day I was on duty with Sam, wearing my tin hat, sat on the roof overlooking London.

The sirens soon sounded, searchlights started beaming up into the sky. They caught a German bomber in their cross beams and the shining aircraft was fired at rapidly by the anti-aircraft guns. It tried to dive and dodge to get out of the searchlight, but without success, the searchlight following it's every move. A big cheer went up from all the surrounding roofs when a lucky hit caused the aircraft to scream down and crash somewhere in the distance.

Waves of planes came over now with bombs crashing all around us. Incendiary bombs fell on the roofs and in the street. We had sandbags that we dropped on the incendiary bombs to put them out. A building about three doors down the road caught fire. I knew there were precious fire engine trailers stored in the basement.

I shouted to Sam, "Come on quick, let's rush down and get those trailers out."

When we got there some other people had already started, and we sweated hard pulling the trailers out into the road, in between dashing to the incendiary bombs that were still raining down, putting them out as quickly as we could. The following morning the road looked a mess, but the trailers were safe.

On the 22nd June 1941 the Germans invaded Russia. We all followed the progress of the battles on the radio and in the papers. We had a map of Russia on the wall in the factory and marked the progress of the armies with little flags. We cheered a lot when at last the Russians started pushing the Germans back.

We got an order to make very heavy waterproof army coats for the Russian army and were now working overtime to produce these coats. We wrote little letters and notes of encouragement and placed them into the overcoat pockets, hoping that someone in Russia understood enough English and would be able to read them.

I had not heard anything from my parents since the invasion of Holland in 1940. In December 1941 I had a letter from my aunt living in America telling me that she had heard that my parents and my brother had been deported to Poland and had most likely been killed in the concentration camp at Lodz Litzmannstadt on arrival.

I was devastated. I had always hoped that when the war was over I would be able to go back to Frankfurt, run up the stairs two at a time to our second floor flat, as I had always done, shouting, "I am home, I am home, Bubie is back." But this was not to be.

I decided I had to get my own back. I was now 19 and I volunteered for the army. I wanted to be involved in the fighting and do my bit. As I was an Eastman cutter producing uniforms I was in a reserved occupation and was not going to be called up, nor of course would I have been as an alien.

When I told my boss Sam that I had volunteered to join the army he said, "You schmock," (Yiddish for idiot) you don't know what you are doing. Too late now and it can't be helped. But when you are in the army and they send you over there keep your head down and make sure you come back home safely."

The Liberation

I joined the training unit in May 1942 and was issued with my first uniform. I immediately inspected the trousers to make sure that the colour matched, and that I had not been issued with a pair bungled by me. Initially, as an alien, I was only allowed to join the 87th Company of the Pioneer Corps.

Map of Lodz Ghetto and Chelmno extermination camp

There were several companies, all with foreigners of Jewish background but also many non-Jews who had fought in the Spanish International Brigade against fascism and could not return to their own country. There were some 10,000 German and Austrian refugees serving in the British forces at that time.

I was first stationed at Pembroke Docks. The barracks, which looked like an old castle, were on top of a hill surrounded by a moat and a wall above it. They formed a complete large square with a parade ground in the centre. At each outer corner was a squared-off outside projection with a manned Bofors anti-aircraft gun. Crossing the bridge over the moat you were faced with a huge studded metal gateway, which could be opened for lorries to enter. Set inside the gateway was a small metal door for personnel access. The guardroom was immediately on the left behind that door, with the duty sergeant sitting immediately by its entrance.

When I reported at the barracks with my kit, straight from the training regiment, I looked so young, that the duty sergeant said, "I didn't know things were so bad that we have to recruit babies now."

My mates overheard this and the nickname 'Baby Face' stuck to me for the rest of the service with the 87th Company.

I was taken to a barrack room with the other three rookies who arrived from the training regiment in Huyton with me; putting my kit on a vacant upper bunk whilst the other three found bunks nearby. I noticed that some soldiers, sitting at the centre table, were unusually quiet and looked very down in the mouth, I joined them and introduced myself. Although they were ex-German and Austrian refugees like myself, we spoke in English.

The Lance Corporal said, "I am Albert, but you will call me Lance Corporal. You are lucky you arrived today. The four bunks you four new recruits have just occupied only became vacant yesterday. The four boys who had been in them were on a landmine training course in a room on the first floor just across the square. For some reason or other, which we have been unable to find out so far, the mine went off and killed all four of them, including Sergeant Wright who was an expert on mines. If you look out of the window over here you can still see the windows, which have been blown out. We are still very upset, so keep the noise down."

We got thorough infantry training. We also had to do some very heavy physical work, working in quarries smashing up stones, building roads and defence lines against a possible German invasion. We were loading and unloading goods wagons, carrying coal or one cwt food sacks of sugar or flour. My knees always buckled when I had to carry these heavy bags.

One of the fringe benefits of working in the quarry was scrounging sticks of dynamite from the engineers. If you dropped one or two sticks of dynamite into the nearby river just above the bend, you could pick up dead or stunned salmon floating on the top by wading into the shallow water. We had a wood-fired stove in the centre of our barrack-room and cooking the fresh salmon on it, late in the evening, giving us a delicious bedtime snack.

During the second week I was on guard duty. At the back of the guardroom we had six cells for prisoners, and often had soldiers from other local regiments in there, awaiting court martial.

Sergeant Bullock called me over and said, "Würzburger, take the prisoner from Cell 4 for a walk round the barracks. He is a conscientious objector from the local infantry regiment. Take your rifle with you and come back in 20 minutes."

I unlocked Cell 4 and marched the prisoner outside. I walked him round the square to one of the outer corners by the anti-aircraft gun. He told me his name was Fred. We sat down, leaning against the wall, and I stood my rifle into a corner. I offered him a cigarette and we started to smoke. I said, "Why are you a conscientious objector? Are you too scared to fight?"

"No fear," he replied, "I just don't believe in killing. My father was in the trenches in the last war and told me all about it. The horror of it all. Men dying by the million on both sides. It was supposed to be the war to finish all wars and here we are fighting the Germans again, just 20 years later, I want nothing to do with it."

"Hang on," I replied, getting quite excited, "This war is quite different from the First World War. I heard all about it from my uncle who served in the German army and was badly wounded at Verdun. You see I am a German Jewish refugee who came to England on my own with a lot of other Jewish children and found freedom in this country. In Germany I was made a second-class citizen in spite of the fact that my father, grandfather, all my forebears and me were born in Germany. My parents and my brother could not leave Germany and they have just been sent to a concentration camp and murdered there. You do not know what it is like to live in Germany under Hitler. Hitler wants to conquer the whole of Europe. He has already occupied the whole of France. We are lucky that he decided to attack the Soviet Union before attacking England. If he ever manages to conquer this country, me and all the other Jews would be exterminated and you and every Englishman would become slave workers for the German master race. We have got to fight for our lives and you must reconsider your decision, stand up and fight this evil with all of us."

Fred sat there stunned, absorbing everything I had said.

We were smoking another cigarette when a voice behind me shouted, "Get up you two and stand to attention." It was the duty officer.

He yelled at the top of his voice for the Guard Commander.

Sergeant Bullock came running round the corner at the double. "Look at these two," he yelled, "Sitting there smoking, with the guard leaving his rifle over there in the corner unattended. Lock up the prisoner and his guard."

"Turn out the guard," yelled the sergeant. They came out at the double. I was marched into the guardroom and was in a cell next to Fred before I could say Jack Robinson, and the duty officer walked off to the officers' mess.

I sat very apprehensively in my cell. My friends on guard brought me loads of mugs of sweet tea. I was wondering whether I would be court-martialled for my offence and how serious it would be judged to be.

Some time after midnight, when I had dozed off on my bunk, the cell door opened and Sergeant Bullock said, "Right, Würzburger, come on out. You are very lucky. I spoke to the duty officer just now when he came out of the officers mess. I told him you had only joined us as a rookie two weeks ago and did not know any better and that no doubt you had learned your lesson. He agreed to let you go and not bring any charges. So pick up your rifle and get back on guard duty."

I thanked him and gratefully rejoined my mates.

I was not doing too well with my guard duties. The next time I was on guard duty we were forming up on the parade ground. The Guard Commander brought us to attention and ordered us to fix bayonets. I had clicked on my bayonet smartly when the next order came, "Present arms, Shoulder Arms." To my horror I heard a loud clatter behind me and saw that the bayonet had shot off my rifle. The Guard Commander yelled at me, "Würzburger, you bloody fool, can't you fit a bayonet properly? If there had been someone behind you, you could have killed the bugger. Go on pick the fucking thing up and fit it on properly, move at the double or I'll put you on a charge."

To the great delight and titter of my mates, I picked up my bayonet, fitted it on properly and jumped back into the ranks and we continued with our changing of the guard parade.

It was my turn to stand on guard, just outside the gate from 10pm to midnight. As all soldiers had to be back in barracks by 10 pm we then closed the heavy studded metal gate, leaving the small door in the gate unlocked, just as I started my guard duty. It was a very dark night and I had to stop and challenge anyone coming across the bridge over the moat. Apart from my rifle I had a torch in my hand and as soon as I heard anyone approach I pointed my rifle and torch in their direction and shouted, "Halt, who goes there?" The person approaching had to stop and reply, using the code word, "Friend." To which I responded, "Advance, friend and be recognised," lowering my rifle and inspecting the arrival with my torch. A few soldiers returned late from the pub, and I had to make sure they reported to the guardroom.

As the night went on fewer and fewer people arrived and I got quite bored. Suddenly I heard the droning noise of some aircraft approaching quite low, some dimmed lights appeared on the water of the inlet. I could now watch the exciting spectacle of two Sunderland flying boats, having come back from an operation, landing precariously on the water. The lights switched off immediately and the following silence was now interrupted by motorboats chugging out to the two Sunderlands barely still visible in the darkness on the water.

Shortly after, I heard someone marching across the bridge. I shouted again, "Halt who goes there?" And got the reply, "Friend." I told him to advance, shining my torch into his face, seeing it was

Lieutenant Brewster. I stepped aside, smartly saluted and was still shining the torch into his face as he returned the salute. He marched on briskly, crashing straight into the studded door. I rushed over and opened the small door for him, shining the torch on the gateway when he yelled, "You idiot, you blinded me with your bloody torch. For God's sake be more careful in the future," storming off. I was relieved at midnight and when I mentioned the incident to the Guard Commander over a mug of tea he laughed out loud saying, "Würzburger, I must say, you take the biscuit, you'll be the bloody death of us all yet."

Early in 1943 the 87th Pioneer Corps was transferred to an engineering camp in Long Marston, near Stratford on Avon. This was a huge camp with a Nissen hut for each section of the Company grouped together. The Royal Engineers occupied a similar group of huts and in the centre were several very large Nissen huts for the Officers Mess, the Sergeants Mess, the cookhouse, the dining room, and the NAAFI, with a parade ground in the centre. A little to one side was an area with small houses for the officers with their families. All these living quarters were near the main entrance, set amongst trees, completely separate from the main area of the camp, which was an immense storage depot for wartime equipment, with many train tracks running in, with wide spaces for loading, unloading and access for lorries between them. We had cranes running on these tracks and also on motorised vehicles.

Our main job was, looking after the various goods stored, checking them and physically handling them in and out, and of course loading and unloading the trains and lorries. The Royal Engineers were keeping the accurate records and decided which was to go where. They drove all the cranes and vehicles and we got on very well with them.

Gary Rogers and Ralph Parker were in the same section with me and my uncle Lawrence, Inge's ex husband, was also in the Company. As he was one of the oldest and a bit fussy, he had been given the nickname 'Aunty'. As we were allowed out every evening, and usually every Saturday afternoon and Sundays he bought himself an old bike soon after we arrived. As it looked that we would be staying at Long Marston for the duration he rented a house in a nearby village for his elderly parents, Max and Betty, so that he could be near them. A few of the older soldiers, who were married, followed suit, bringing their wives near the camp.

Gary, Ralph and I became very friendly and often went to Stratford together, sometimes by train from the station next door to the camp, on the back of a lorry or by bike. In the spring and summer we hired boats on the river, cruising up and down, picking up service girls, whenever we could. We took trunks with us so we could swim in the river and had the time of our lives. Sometimes it seemed to us that there wasn't a war on because we were so carefree, enjoying ourselves immensely. Of course we went to pubs and drank too much. There were plenty of Military Police about keeping us in order, and Alf, another mate of ours, was booked for 'urinating in the Streets of Stratford' and given 7 days C.B. (confined to barracks), because he had been too drunk to find the public toilet.

For me the best of our entertainment was the chance to go to the Stratford Theatre, which was open during the Spring and Summer to see many Shakespeare plays beautifully performed. Soldiers were allowed in at the special rate of one shilling and we could sit whereever we wanted. Watching a play one day a message was passed to the King that thousands of French had been slain, but not a single Englishman had been lost. Like one we all shouted in unison, "Lies, lies, bloody lies, don't believe a word of this communiqué!" The cast just paused a moment, bowed to us and continued.

Ralph Parker

When on duty, we all worked very hard, the older soldiers were content, feeling that they were doing their bit, but us younger ones, we were wanting to do so much more, then just helping the war effort.

I was very proud to wear the British uniform, especially when on leave in London, mingling with all the other British soldiers. As the Germans achieved more and more successes and occupied ever more countries, I felt very strongly that I wanted to do much more. I wanted to be in the fighting. I wanted to defeat Fascism and the Nazis. I wanted to liberate the occupied countries. I felt frustrated and ashamed that I was still in England, whilst millions of British soldiers fought in the battlefields.

At last I got my chance. In the summer of 1943 it was announced that anyone wishing to join a fighting unit would be allowed to do so. I immediately volunteered, was interviewed and to my delight my application was accepted. I was given an intelligence test and selected for the Royal Tank Regiment. It was suggested to me to change my name from Karl Robert Würzburger to an English name in case I was taken prisoner. As my initials KRW were on all my kit, I had to keep these initials and decided on a very common English name Kenneth Robert Ward by going through the telephone directory searching for a surname starting with Wa. I wanted the 'a' so I would at least be the first of the 'Ws' to be called out on pay parade. Additionally, it had to be short for simple signatures, and a very common name, so that I would not stand out in the crowd. My army number was changed at the same time from 13807502 to 13118379. I was issued with a new Pay book and a new dog tag, which had to be worn round the neck. On this tag was my name and number and in the centre the letter 'J' to indicate my religion, so that if I was killed in action I would be buried in the right grave. I immediately decided, that should I ever be taken prisoner by the Germans I would have to lose it as the 'J' indicated that I was Jewish and I would no doubt then be shot.

In September 1943 I was transferred to the 55th Training Regiment RAC at Farnborough, together with thirty of my comrades. We started a very rigorous and intensive training for four months. It was a very hard, disciplined training, ranging from square bashing, driving, map reading, radio operating and gunnery, to the ultimate delight of tank driving and firing a tank gun on the firing range. The training sergeants and staff wondered, why we as Germans, were willing and very keen, to fight our own countrymen. I explained to them that Germany is not my country any more, after what they had done to me, that I was fighting fascism, a vile Nazi dictatorship. I had to explain this many more times, when I had joined my regiment.

My 21st birthday was on the 29th November 1943. I mentioned it to Sergeant Walker, in charge of our troop, who said, "Great, we must celebrate this in the pub tonight, I will bring along the SQMS and we will meet you and a couple of your mates at the gate at 7pm tonight." I was overjoyed and asked Ralph and Gary to come along.

We put on our best gear, met the Sergeant and the SQMS and I walked proudly across to the pub. The Sergeant said, "Many happy returns on your birthday, the 21st is a great occasion and a big celebration is called for. I will have a pint of bitter and I know the SQMS will have a pint of Guinness, you better ask Parker and Rogers what they want." They both smiled and gave me their orders, and I dutifully went to the bar and got the drinks. We had a great evening, which cost Ralph, Gary and me a fortune because neither the Sergeant nor the SQMS bought a single drink and started to switch to the more expensive shorts.

On one of the map reading and wireless training exercises I was in a P.U. together with Ralph, which had been fitted with one of the 19 sets, the radios we were going to use on the tanks when in action. We were given a map reference to go to two tracks crossing in a dense forest. We had no difficulty finding it, when Jack the driver said, "Before you report in let's drive back to the café we passed down the road. We can park there and have a cuppa whilst you come up on the air to get your further instructions." No sooner said than done. Ralph and Jack went into the café to order the tea and I came up on the 19 set reporting our position, but giving the map reference we had been asked to proceed to. The wireless instructor came up on the air, "Roger, stand by for further instructions. Over and out." I now nipped into the café to have my cup of tea and asked Ralph to go into the P.U. to stand by for any messages. I had only settled down for a few minutes when the Corporal wireless instructor drove up, rushed in and said, "Listen

Ken as a soldier

boys, this is not your map reference, you can't bloody well fool me, and if you ever try this lark again I will put you on a charge. Now go and get me a cup of tea and a slice of toast, and be quick about it, and then you will take me to the rendezvous point given to you on the map reference, and you'd better be right."

We also had to endure petty unnecessary discomforts during our four months training in the Training Regiment in Farnborough. One of the tasks before being passed out and sent to your fighting regiment was to complete a 10-mile route march with rifle and a very heavy full kit, in under two hours. I failed two attempts and on the third one my best friend in the army, Gary Rogers, who was also a P.T. instructor accompanied me on his bike, urging me on and on, saying, "Come on Ken, you will make it this time because you must make it or you will be left behind here and not be able to join a fighting unit with us."

"It's alright for you," I moaned, "you are on a bike and in a P.E. kit and I have all this bloody lot to carry." Did I make it? Of course not, although I made the best time of all the three attempts, by collapsing across the finishing line after 2 hours and 2 minutes. Now I was desperate and practically in tears. I thought I would be left behind, that I would have to stay on and miss the second front.

To this day I do not know why I got my posting to the 1st RTR together with all my mates. Did Sergeant Walker who saw me cross the finishing line feel sorry for me, did Gary put in a good word for me, or did the 1st RTR need men so desperately for the D-day landing that they broke the rules?

I joined the 1st RTR in January 1944 on their return from Italy, in Brandon near Thetford. We were soon issued with new tanks and training commenced with all the new equipment. I was allocated to a crew in 7 troop of A Squadron and we had a Sherman tank with a 17-pounder tank gun, called The Firefly. It was the most powerful tank gun in the British army, nearly equal to the dreaded German 88.

Our Squadron Leader was Major Bob Crisp, who was a South African champion bowler. He had just come back from Africa and Italy. He was very easy going and friendly as was the Regimental Commander Col. Mike Carver, the youngest colonel in the British army at that time, who later became Field Marshal Lord Carver. Neither of them stuck to the usual British army discipline, talking to us ordinary troopers on practically equal terms, although they expected their orders to be followed implicitly when we were out on training, driving the tanks across the countryside and through the forests, learning to map read and keep radios on net.

They tried very hard to perfect my English for communicating over the air. One of the phrases used at the end of a message was, "Roger, wilco out" which meant 'Message understood, will comply with the order, end of message' I used to pronounce the 'w' like a 'v'. It was pointed out to me that the Germans would be listening in to our radio communications and if they could identify a voice speaking on the air they would then realise when a regiment had moved its position. I used to sit in the barracks and practise to my friend Ralph

Gary Rogers

saying repeatedly, "Roger, wilco out – roger wilco out" to the great amusement of anyone listening.

Instead of wearing ties the two officers wore knotted scarves, sticking out of their greatcoats. Col. Carver had a mild stammer; similar to that of King George V, who came himself to inspect us shortly before D-day. We were all on parade, waiting for the King to arrive. Ralph and I were in the rear column and had a small pocket chess with us, quietly playing a game.

Suddenly Ralph said the King and the colonel were approaching. I wonder whether the King has been warned that Mike has got this small stammer and if not, what he will say when Mike asks him, "Your Ma-majesty, wouwould you like a dridrink in thethe mess?" Will the King bash him one and say: "Whowho dodo you think, youyou are talking toto?"

Tank crew in action on our Firefly
from left: Eric Marsland (gunner) Ken Ward (wireless operator)
Charles Adams (driver)

We both laughed quietly and stood smartly to attention as Col. Carver was leading the King past us. I had never seen the King in person before.

Shortly after the King's inspection we were told that Field Marshall Montgomery was going to inspect us and give us a briefing about D-day. We had all been irritated when all our leave had been stopped because the invasion was imminent.

The night before Monty arrived, we painted in large white letters on the tanks, parked in the field in which we were going to be inspected, the words NO LEAVE – NO SECOND FRONT. The officers were not pleased when they saw this in the morning but it was too late to clean off the tanks before his arrival.

The whole regiment had assembled in the field, when Monty arrived in a Jeep. He got out, jumped on the bonnet and slid off his Jeep coat, revealing rows and rows of medals to approving sounds from the whole of the crowd. He addressed us in a very loud voice, "Alright boys, sit down." He waited for us to sit down on the grass and continued, "It's good to see you all again, and I am proud to be fighting the Boche with you now in Europe. There is one thing I am going to tell you right now and that is you will not be getting any leave but you will be getting a second front so you can put that in your pipe and smoke it. The second front is imminent. You will be expected to fight at your best and there will be casualties but we will succeed, and we will defeat and destroy the enemy. We will give no quarter and we will only accept unconditional surrender. You will be given your orders when you have embarked. Good luck boys and I will see you next over there."

We were very impressed with his speech, and stood up as one and cheered as he was driven off in his jeep.

One day I was in the shower on my own, singing in a loud tenor voice the very popular Russian song, 'Fatherland of mine so free and…' I made up the words to sound Russian as I was singing, when Albala, a refugee from Turkey walked in, got under a shower next to me, with me continuing to sing quite undisturbed.

When I finished he said, "That was great Ken, you have got a lovely voice, I never knew you speak Russian. I could not quite understand the lyrics, so perhaps you let me have them later, as I would like to memorise them."

Montgomery inspecting troops

I was dumbfounded and never had the courage to tell him, that I had just made up the words and that they were only gibberish.

Now came the time to waterproof our tanks so we could drive off the LSTs straight through the water if the ship could not get close enough to the beach to open its ramp straight onto the sand. Each tank crew was issued with the necessary kit and instructions. The aim was to waterproof the tanks halfway up to the turret. It meant bolting on a square upright box to the back of the tank, with the exhaust pipes running in to it. As we had to seal the area between the body of the tank and the turret, we would be unable to use the traversing gear and fire any of the guns on landing. We installed explosive charges under the waterproofing so that we could blow it all off as soon as we hit the beach.

This was an enormous task, which was expected to take about a week. The whole 22nd Armoured Brigade moved to Orwell Park, halfway between Brandon and Felixstowe, where we were scheduled to embark for the invasion of the heavily defended continent and would have to break through the German West Wall to get a foothold inland.

We had taken over a large residential private preparatory school that had been evacuated by the staff and pupils, and requisitioned by the M.o.D.

I did not know then that the future Headmaster of Orwell Park School, Mr Andrew Auster, and parents of the school pupils would erect on the 15th September 2001 a Memorial Plaque to us, the 22nd Armoured Brigade, in the school grounds. They also arranged for surviving members to meet there in September each year over dinner to exchange reminiscences. Mr. Auster even organised, in association with a former parent, David Eagle, for his own tank to be there to greet us at the main entrance.

At that first reunion, to my horror, I realised that I was now unable to run up the side of the tank, getting inside in no time, like I used to do. We showed the pupils over the tank, told them about our experiences, and were rewarded later with superb musical performances put on for our entertainment and an excellent dinner. Rod Scott exhibited other memorabilia from his personal museum.

Nor did I know then that the Thetford Forest Desert Rats Association, Chairman Rod Scott, would erect a memorial to the Desert Rats bearing a Cromwell tank brought back from the Normandy battlefields, in Brandon forest on the exact site where we had been stationed to receive our new tanks and training for the D-day landings, and where we had been inspected by the late King George V and Field Marshall Montgomery.

It was a long journey from Brandon and I was very impressed when we drove with our tanks through the school gates and saw the long, imposing building at the top of the slope.

I said to Les, the tank commander, "This is great, we will be in lovely quarters here."

"You'll be so bloody lucky. That will be the officers quarters and brigade and Squadron H.Q. We are driving round the back, following the troop leader, and find a space at the bottom of the field,

Orwell Park School

where the tanks will be parked and waterproofed. We will have to kip next to the tanks. I have been told that there will be a cookhouse for each of the three regiments in one of the buildings. At least we will be fed whilst we work and don't have to do our own cooking. Once we have parked up, I want you to walk up to the buildings and find out where our cookhouse is and what time they are serving up. I am starving and can do with a meal."

The waterproofing went fairly smoothly and more quickly than anticipated, with a lot of assistance from the Royal Engineers, so we had extra days of relaxing in the beautiful grounds before leaving this lovely location.

I was now very sad and frightened wondering what the future would hold as we left Orwell Park School at the end of May 1944 to embark on an LST at Felixstowe on June1st. As we drove through the town of Felixstowe towards the harbour, young children and women were running alongside the

Pupils, veterans and tank at Orwell Park School
14 September 2006

tanks, calling out to us, cheering us on by shouting,
"Good luck, give the b.....d Jerries what for and
come back safely."

Ken at Memorial Plaque at Orwell Park School

Ken on Sherman Firefly tank at Orwell Park School
RTR Annual Reunion

I realised I might not be coming back and would not need the money I had in my pocket and threw it down to the children who whooped with joy when they saw the coins spilling on to the pavement.

I called out to the other members of my crew, "Come on, throw your money to the kids, we won't need it when we land over there."

The boys on the other tanks realised what we were doing and joined us in throwing money to the waving crowd.

The harbour was black with landing craft right on the quay, with others waiting further out to berth, with destroyers and different types of warships laying offshore, protecting the invasion fleet with hundreds of barrage balloons floating in

Thetford Desert Rat Memorial

the air. There was a huge traffic jam, which the harbour master and his officers were frantically trying to sort out.

The squadron kept very closely together and we followed our troop, which was finally directed onto an LST. We drove up the ramp straight into the hold and were directed by a member of the ship's crew to the other end, parking right against the closed ramp at the far end of the ship. It was very dark, smelt of fumes, and there was a lot of clanging of chains as the crew secured the tanks to heavy metal rings let into the floor. We rushed upstairs into the quarters with our bedding rolls to secure a bunk

As the ship was very overcrowded I did not manage to get a bunk with my crew so I had to sleep in my bedding roll on the floor next to them. An American crew manned this LST and we got excellent fresh food, which we had not been used to. I was always seasick when on a small pleasure boat or fishing trip going out to sea so I was quite apprehensive in case I should get seasick on the crossing being very aware of the bad weather we were having and noticing the considerable swell of the sea inside the harbour. I need not have worried, because the MO on board walked around dispensing a special supply of seasick tablets. They worked like a charm and I was able to eat and enjoy the American cuisine without any side affects.

We remained outside the harbour for a few days in a heavy swell. I stood near the bow of the ship with the rest of my crew when the fleet started steaming away and Les said, "Well boys, here we go again. Churchill will stick up his two fingers as usual in the 'V' for victory sign, which means of course, 'the war will go on for another two years', let's go and have a piss up whilst we can and play a game of cards."

We were informed that we were heading for Normandy and would land on Gold Beach. The sea was quite rough as we approached the beach. There was a lot of shelling from the shore batteries and the big battleships lying off the beach. There were thousands of ships on the channel opposite the Normandy coast with each ship carrying barrage balloons so that the channel now looked like the defences of London. Flights of bombers were continuously droning overhead towards the French coast, with Spitfires flying in and around the ships defending us from the Messerschmitts and the individual German Dornier bombers that were trying to have a go at the battleships.

We were told to be ready to land after lunch. We strapped all our bedding and equipment on the back of the tank and rushed up to the canteen for a quick last lunch. We were all quite tense but I tried not to show it as I was the only one in the crew who had not yet been in battle. As the LST slowly approached the beach we went into the hold and mounted our tank. There was a smell of oil and fumes in the air and we could hear the shelling, with shells landing on the beach from inside the hull. We were then told that the LST could not get right up to the beach but that we would be ferried across on a small flat ferry and would have to drive off the ferry and the rest of the way through the water with our waterproofed gear, as soon as we were told to do so.

Charlie was in his driving seat, revving up the engine. I had switched on the radio making sure we were on net, speaking to the radio operator of the Troop Leader's tank, and then stood on my seat so that my body was halfway out. Les, the tank commander also stood on his seat to get a good view and Jimmy, the gunner, stood on the side at the back of the tank so that he could detonate the waterproofing, as soon as we were on shore.

Suddenly there was a lot of clanging and chain rattling as the front of the LST opened up and the front ramp came down. The Ferry was already there, the plate appeared to clang on to it and as we were first in line, we drove on to the flat ferry, which shuddered under our weight and drove as far forward as we could, to allow another tank to get on.

We then closed in on the beach and had to drive through about five feet of water before getting the tracks onto dry land. Jimmy blew some of the waterproofing off, getting inside the turret on his seat and blew off the rest of the waterproofing, testing the turret traversing gear to make sure it was still functioning. I had landed at last as a member of my tank crew in Normandy on D+1

As we moved up the beach the Troop Leader came up on the B set (which is short range only to speak to the Troop Commander) telling us to quickly move towards the right where there was a small lane leading off it and to drive up to the end until he had caught up. The beach was littered with knocked out tanks and vehicles. There was a First Aid Station at the side with medics moving the wounded on to stretchers. The houses on the cliff above were already flying French flags. I took it all in, with wonderment, with one of the earphones clipped tightly to my ear and the other free to listen to what was going on. As we approached the entrance to the lane, I heard a binging noise, and noticed that Les had disappeared inside the tank, and that the men in the other tanks following us had also disappeared.

I slipped inside the tank, standing on the floor, when Les said, "I wondered when you would come in, we have been sniped at for the last few minutes from somewhere on top of the cliff."

I had learned my first lesson; don't be too cocky in battle and keep your head down.

Now I had reached my objective I was a fighting soldier. I had at last a chance to revenge my parents and my brother. I would not take any German prisoners.

Then I learned my second lesson. Two days after we had landed, we were parked in a lane near a

Firefly landing on a Normandy beach

hedge. As things were reasonably quiet, we brewed up a cup of tea behind the tank. Suddenly there was some movement on the side and a German soldier crawled out from under the hedge. He looked very old, dishevelled and dirty. He stood there with his hands up, trembling and very frightened. He had obviously been in that ditch since the previous day. I looked into his eyes and could see his fear; that he expected to be shot. All my resolutions were immediately forgotten. I felt compassion for this frightened human being and gave him a mug of our compo tea.

Shortly after that I saw a poem by a Russian soldier to his girlfriend Valentina Serova, printed in one of the daily papers delivered with the rations and which affected me very deeply, making me cry, because I had no one waiting for me:

Wait for me, and I'll come back!

Konstantin Simonov (1941)

Wait for me, and I'll come back!
Wait with all you've got!
Wait, when dreary yellow rains
Tell you, you should not
Wait when snow is falling fast.
Wait when summer's hot,
Wait when yesterdays are past,
Others are forgot.
Wait when from that far-off place,
Letters don't arrive.
Wait, when those with whom you wait
Doubt if I'm alive.

Wait for me, and I'll come back!
Wait in patience yet
When they tell you off by heart
That you should forget.
Even when my dearest ones
Say that I am lost,
Even when my friends give up,
Sit and count the cost,
Drink a glass of bitter wine

To the fallen friend –
Wait! And do not drink with them
Wait until the end!

Wait for me and I'll come back,
Dodging every fate!
"Wait a bit of luck!" they'll say,
Those that did not wait.
They will never understand
How amidst the strife,
By your waiting for me, dear,
You had saved my life.
How I made it, we shall know,
Only you and I.
You alone knew how to wait –
We alone know why!

At night, when sleeping in my bedding roll either next to the tank, underneath the tank or inside it, hearing all the German shells landing near us, with planes droning overhead and bombs bursting in the fields, I said silent little prayers, "Please my God, don't let me get injured and don't let me die yet, I am still so young, there are so many things I have not seen or experienced yet, I have never ever made love to a woman, I have never seen a television broadcast, please do not let me die, before I have experienced and seen more of life."

Charlie Adams, our driver, had joined the army shortly before the war broke out. He had signed on for seven years and five years reserve and had been sent over to France during the phoney war. When the Germans attacked through Holland and Belgium he had to abandon his tank leaving all his equipment behind but managed to get on to one of the little boats coming out to rescue our soldiers at Dunkirk

Back in England, he rejoined the 1st Royal Tank Regiment with other survivors and new recruits, and was sent, after being re-equipped, to Africa. There they battled backwards and forwards until finally they broke through at El-Alamein, fighting their way again right across Africa. Then came the Sicilian campaign followed by the landing in Italy at Salerno. Charlie drove his tank all the way up to Monte Massico and Mondragone and fought his last action in Italy at Cicola. From there they came back to England to be re-equipped once again for the Normandy invasion. That's when I first met Charlie.

When the war finally ended Charlie was one of the first to be demobbed as he had served his seven years. But he was soon recalled as a reservist when the Korean trouble started only to die miserably of dysentery in a Korean prisoner-of-war camp leaving behind a wife with a disabled son.

Jimmy Hague was our gunner when I first joined the crew at Brandon and Les Allen the sergeant tank commander. Both had been through the same actions as Charlie and I was as green as you can make them and was learning the hard way.

After the disaster at Villers Bocage on the 11th June where Albala was the first of my friends to be killed. We lost tanks even though we were in reserve. We were surprised by two Tigers who came suddenly out of some dense shrubbery to our right. I spotted them first, and yelled to Les, who directed Jimmy onto the target. Jimmy started firing straight away and I was busy loading the gun with A.P. shots. We fired on the move, hitting one of the tanks, but did not knock it out, but obviously disabling it, as they did not fire back.

Fortunately the Germans were as surprised by the encounter as we had been, because the second tank did not start firing immediately they saw us, although their powerful 88 mm guns were pointing straight at us. No doubt they had never seen a British tank with such a long gun before. By the time the gunner of the second Tiger recovered his wits and started firing at us we were moving so fast that both shots missed us.

However, having such a very long barrel proved to be a disadvantage. We were travelling at speed, with the gun sticking out sideways, and hit a tree with the end of the gun barrel. The impact smashed the traversing gear, and the turret span like a top at a terrific pace. Fortunately I was standing on the lip of the footrest of my seat and not on the turret floor, or my feet would have been cut off.

We swung round behind a copse for cover, and continued to move back as fast as we could. When we got back to the regiment, we had to wait to get a tank replacement. Jimmy was transferred to another crew whilst we waited for our tank. Eric

Knocked-out British armour

Marsland, who was also an old campaigner, replaced him.

Colonel Mike Carver was highly liked and respected by all the troops serving under him and proved again and again why this was the case. Whilst we were on stand-by to take the very heavily defended town of Caen the colonel received an order from Brigade H.Q to take a particular outlying village. Mike requested air and artillery support. When he was told that this was not available he came up on the air, "No air support, no artillery support, no village, over and out." We did not go in, as the colonel was not prepared to waste lives.

On the following day we were parked behind a hedge, near a hillock, with German tanks and infantry behind the hedges across a field. We were inside our tank awaiting orders to advance, with the hatches half closed, as there was a lot of shelling

Ken's Firefly tank in action
Les Allen, Tank Commander and Charlie Adams, driver

and small arms fire and the occasional airburst, an high explosive shell (H.E.), set to explode in the air above tanks to kill the crews.

Suddenly I heard a jeep arrive, pulling up behind us. Mike jumped out and walked briskly up the hillock, ignoring all the shelling and watched the Germans through his binoculars from behind a hedge. He turned, ran down the slope back to his jeep, waving to us as he passed. I felt a bit sheepish, opened my hatch, sticking my head out again to be able to see better, and to be able to wave back. We soon got orders to advance, clearing the German infantry out of the field, after the tanks had withdrawn.

On the 17th July 1944 we moved from orchards surrounding Jerusalem to concentrate on the attack on Caen. We were briefed that it was a city very heavily defended by the experienced SS Panzer

Lehr Division and additional strong armour and SS infantry, as from there the roads opened to the West. We were told we would be given a lot of artillery and air support.

Les immediately said, "The bleedin buggers. I have heard all this bullshit before, what they are really telling us is that this will be a lengthy, difficult and bloody battle. Well, here we go."

We moved on and ended up on a hillside, overlooking Caen. We had a clear view of the town spreading out in front of us. There was a lot of shelling going on from both sides. The Germans using their Nebelwerfer, which fired a large number of shells, from a rotating drum, all hitting the ground practically at the same time. We stayed well inside the tank, just occasionally jumping out to brew up a cup of tea behind the tank, making do with our hard dog biscuits, tinned butter and some tinned spam, which we made up inside the tank. We waited for the early hours of the morning, when the air attack started. Hundreds of planes came over, flying in formation, bombing the town. In practically no time Caen was flattened and I could not see how anybody could have possibly survived in the town.

We moved in with our tanks, accompanied by infantry, and found that a large number of Germans had survived the bombing and artillery barrage, which was now laying down a barrage further ahead of us. We drew a lot of fire from the infantry, who knocked out some of our tanks with their bazookas.

The SS Panzer Lehr Division had withdrawn behind the hills at the other side of the town. We followed and left the infantry to clear Caen of the remaining German pockets, pulling up in some fields the other side of Caen, knowing that the German tanks were not far in front of us, being heavily shelled by our artillery. We managed to cook a meal behind the tank, but took it inside to eat. Having been confined all this time inside the tank, I needed to relieve myself badly. As most of the shelling was by us towards the German lines I took the opportunity to grab our shovel and dash across to a hedge, dug a little hole, sat down and finished unhindered. Just as I had pulled up my trousers I heard a shell coming over. I sprinted like mad across 50 yards of the field, which had just recently been ploughed up and was crouching half way up the tank, when the shell exploded right next to me, with shell splinters hitting the outside of the tank all around me. I could not believe my luck, when I managed to duck inside the tank, just as the next shell landed. Les smiled at me and said, "You lucky bastard, thank God you managed to bring back the shovel."

The battle continued for a few days with us advancing slowly, losing a few tanks when we were positioned on top of a hill, with the sun setting down behind us, making us a clear target. But we got our own back, when the sun rose in the morning behind a row of German tanks, clearly illuminating them against the skyline. We opened up and knocked out four tanks before they could move back behind cover. By now the Division was considerably below strength, the infantry and the tanks having had a trying time taking Caen and we went for a rest and re-fitment back into the nearby Gaumont area.

Our squadron pulled up into a leaguer in a field, the tanks as usual forming a square, with the soft vehicles in the centre. The supplies of compo boxes had arrived and been stored away and we had filled up with petrol. Charlie cooked our meal on a five-gallon drum, from which we had removed the top and bottom and which had two metal bars running across near the top end, on which we placed the frying pan and the billycan for boiling water for compo tea. This was a ready mixed tea with milk powder and sugar and it had taken me about a week to get used to its taste. He poured petrol liberally into the oil drum and lit the fire and opened a tin of skinless sausages, which were about the vilest food in the compo box of rations for 14 men. We got two boxes per week for our crew of 4 men. In each box was also a tin of sweets and chocolates, and we took it in turns to send every other tin home, as chocolates and sweets were on ration.

I had just been given the nickname of Buzz, because I have very large ears and there had been a cartoon in the Daily Mirror showing a man, with one large ear cocked to the sky, listening out for German buzz bombs, which were now arriving over London. This was a pilotless plane loaded with high explosive. When it reached its target, the engine, which sounded like a motorbike chugging along loudly, cut out, diving to the ground and exploding on impact. If you could hear the engine cutting out you just had enough time to run for cover.

After we had eaten I went to the long metal box at the back of the tank in which we kept our rations and took out some Camembert, which I had swapped with a French farmer for a tin of bully beef. I put some of the cheese on the hard compo biscuits, which we carried. It was nice, soft and runny and Eric said, "Hey Buzz, you can't eat them, that cheese has gone off, just smell the food locker, it stinks to high heaven from that bloody cheese."

I laughed out loud, realising that Eric had never seen any Camembert before, saying, "Come on Eric, it's fine, it is just ripe, try a little, I am sure you will like it."

He tried half a biscuit of mine, "Yes, Buzz, it's not too bad, I might just get to like it."

He did in the end, but neither Les nor Charlie were ever prepared to eat that cheese.

As there was more shelling during the evening we fortunately decided to sleep inside the tank. About midnight a single German Messerschmitt flew low over our leaguer dropping one anti-personnel bomb hitting a petrol lorry in the centre of the square, which went straight up in flames. A flight of American bombers high up in the sky spotted our formation of tanks, well lit up by the burning petrol lorry, and dropped their load of bombs on us. Several crew members, who were sleeping in their bedding rolls next to their tanks, were killed or injured.

Les shouted at the planes, high above, which had already moved on, "You f...ing idiots can't you see the white stars painted on the back of our tanks?"

The following morning we moved further forward. As things were very quiet Eric said over

108

the intercom, "Come on Buzz, give us one of your Itie songs over the radio," as I had done many times before. I loved singing and hearing my voice in our earphones and started singing 'Oh Solo Mio' and 'Torna Soriento' when a furious voice came over the 'B' set, "For Christ sake stop that singing, whoever it is. You are jamming all the bloody communication on the main set."

I listened in, looked at the set and realised that it had been switched to the A set, which was the main communication channel for the whole of the squadron. They were not at all pleased.

We then started moving forward through the Fallaise gap into Lisieux encountering numbers of dead soldiers and cattle on the roads, smashed up villages, trees with their branches sticking up forlornly into the sky, desolation everywhere.

At last our breakthrough succeeded and the regiment advanced very fast towards the Seine. I was again happily singing one of my favourite Italian songs at the top of my voice but on the intercom this time when Charlie suddenly pulled the tank up to the side of the road and stopped. He popped out of his hatch above the driving seat, came up to the turret and told Les and myself, "We have had it, the clutch has burned out, we can't move another inch."

Les immediately reported this to the Troop Leader. Everyone climbed happily out of the tank, and I was left up top on wireless watch.

After about twenty minutes the Squadron Leader came up on the air, "A7C, we are advancing very fast and you will soon be out of wireless range. Don't worry you are on the centre line of the advance and tank transporters will pick you up soon. Good luck, over and out."

I gave the message to Les and we started cooking a meal. Quite a lot of tanks had passed by us but then there was silence. The radio set had stopped crackling and I could not hear any more messages. The 19 set had only a range of 15 miles, and the regiment must have advanced well past that. By nightfall there had been no more movement along our road for hours.

Les said, "Great, the bastards changed the centre line and nothing else will come down this road."

We got out a bottle of Calvados, which we had been given by a French farmer, to calm our nerves, and were joined by a group of French marquis who had been searching the outlaying copses for stray German soldiers. So now we were on our own. We took it in turns to be on guard that night and the

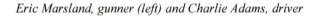

Eric Marsland, gunner (left) and Charlie Adams, driver

following night, as we were afraid that there might still be some German infantry milling about.

At last we heard the rumble of some heavy vehicles and had the welcome sight of three tank transporters coming down the road. They stopped by our tank and the sergeant in charge was very surprised to see us, "We are always driving along, searching to recover knocked out tanks, but I have never yet come across a tank with a crew standing by it. What's the matter, mates, had enough of the war?"

Les replied, "No, the bloody clutch has burned out and the regiment has swanned along so fast that we are out of wireless range and haven't got a clue of what has been going on."

"Of course you are out of range, we have not only advanced very fast, we are well across the Seine by now. Tell you what we will do, I will take you all back to our forward workshop somewhere near Amiens and we can put a new clutch in for you, and then you can be on your way to rejoin your regiment.

We arrived in the depot that evening. The officer in charge made us very welcome and allocated us to sleep in a hut and arranged for us to have dinner in the mess. He got in touch with our Regimental Head Quarters (RHQ), told them where we were, that a new clutch would be fitted the following day and that we could be off the day after.

After we had a lovely hot shower Eric said, "Come on Buzz, you speak the lingo, let's all go into town and have a look around, make sure we take our French francs along, which we have been issued with."

We set off, walking along and looking down a side street Charlie spotted a red light outside a bar. "Jesus, look, I bet that's a brothel, let's have a shufty."

We walked across, entering the dingy-looking, premises. It consisted of a very large room, with comfortable chairs and tables along one side and a big bar on the other. There were about eight or ten men sitting at some of the tables with scantily dressed women. We sat down and I got a round of beers from the bar. As we started drinking four pretty girls ambled over and joined us. They spoke hardly any English. One of the girls said to Les, "Jigge, jigge jig, tres bons." They all smiled at him and took him to the brothel ma, sitting at a till at the bottom of the stairs, where he had to pay some money and disappeared up the stairs.

Charlie said, "Come on Buzz, now is your chance to lose your virginity, have a go."

Having said that, he disappeared with the other girl.

Eric said smiling, "This is great, I haven't had sex since I have last been home and feel as randy as anything. Go on Buzz, have a go."

The very attractive girl sitting next to me only wore a pair of shorts and a flimsy blouse, which was half unbuttoned showing most of her firm white breasts. She was running her hand along the inside of my thighs. I had never experienced anything like that before and got very aroused. As we walked up the stairs, after I had paid the madam, the girl said to me in French, "Is this the first time you are making love?"

I blushed and replied, "No, no, I have made love many times."

We entered a room, she stripped off naked and laid on the bed. I stared in wonderment at her beautiful body and as she opened her legs wide, I saw for the first time a vagina. I stripped off quickly, she beckoned me across, slid a condom on my penis and we made love violently.

I did not want to stop after my first orgasm, but she patted me on the shoulder saying, "This is enough," no doubt realising that I had never made love before. She took me over to a hand washbasin and gently washed my private parts. As we came down the stairs I was greeted with clapping and riotous cheers from my crew.

They finished putting the clutch in the following evening and took us on a tank transporter to Brussels, where we stayed the night, and which had only been liberated on the 3rd September. Having received our orders, we rejoined the regiment at Malines, a few miles Northeast of Brussels.

On arrival I heard that the Jewish Brigade was in a tent encampment in the field next to us. I asked Les if I could go and have a look to see if my brother was there and he said, "Yes, but be quick, because we may be moving off soon."

Eric decided to come with me. I looked around amongst the Jewish soldiers and asked one of them, "Do you know Paul Würzburger?"

I struck lucky, as he indicated a tent, and said, "I think he is in there."

We rushed over to the tent, I called out his name and could not believe my eyes when I saw Paul getting up, turn round and look at me, "Bubie", he called out, "Bubie, is it really you?"

We embraced; we had not seen each other for over five years. "Mensch" he said, breaking partly into German "You have grown up." Looking at my black beret and at Eric he said unbelievingly, "You are in the tanks?"

"Yep" I replied, "I landed on D+1 in Normandy and it is great to meet you here. This is Eric, a Yorkshireman, my mate and our gunner. It is fantastic to see you here, looking so well. Now we can communicate with each other through the army mail, I am in the 1st R.T.R. and my name is now Ward and I will write to you. But we must dash now. Our regiment is about to leave. Our tanks are just the other side of your field. Come to the gate with us and see us off."

As the three of us ran to the gate, we were stared at by the soldiers of the Jewish Brigade, who had just arrived here, having fought their way up through Italy. On the run Paul said, "I have changed my name too, I am not Paul any more, a German name, I am now known as Daniel."

We reached the gate, embraced once more, with my brother watching us running across to our tank and mounting it.

1st RTR in Holland 10th November 1944 to 21st February 1945

When we came to Oosterhout we were stood down and told that the Poles were going to put in an attack that night, and that we should take no notice of any shooting. As we had been in action for some time, we parked near a private house owned by Mr Korput, who made us very welcome, and the whole crew slept in the lounge or dining room. We were so dirty, that only after we had a wash did the Korput's realise that we were white, as on arrival they thought we were Negroes.

The family were very nice and friendly. They had kept a pig, which they slaughtered in our honour and we had fresh meat and black pudding for the first time in a very long time. They were over the moon to have been liberated and to be free and absolutely hated the Rotmuffe (Dutch slang for Germans).

There was a sweet factory nearby, which had only been allowed to supply Germany, but now that the Germans had gone, the factory was able to supply all the Dutch people.

There was a lot of shelling and fighting going on during the night, but we took no notice. On the following morning we were told that the Poles had indeed put an attack in that night, but it had been a Polish division, fighting for the Germans. Our infantry had therefore to defend Oosterhout without our help, as we had been given the wrong orders.

At Christmas 1944 we were sent to Sittard. We dug the tanks in as we expected a counter attack by the Germans. It was so cold that you could not touch the outside of the tank without gloves on as it would have burnt your skin off. The Germans were east of us, just the other side of Tüddern. As we were short of infantry we had to man foxholes on guard in the forward area. On Christmas Day I could hear the Germans singing Christmas carols in a house across the field from where I was in a foxhole. No shots were fired that day. This was a very emotional and frightening experience for me.

In January 1945 Les Allen had taken over a different tank and Oscar, who had arrived fresh from home, replaced him. On the 18th January 1945 we advanced into Echt and subsequently Schilberg and were straddled down the main street. Our troop advanced to a crossroad and turned right, moving up about three hundred yards. We were told to stop at a junction whilst the rest of the troop advanced further. Our infantry boys occupied the houses on either side of the road. The radio crackled, telling us of fighting in close proximity. Suddenly the three tanks of our troop returned at great speed, driving past us without stopping. The troop leader ordering us to stay and shoot up any enemy tanks that might be following.

The infantry boys, who had been occupying the houses on either side, withdrew leaving us on our own. The shelling and small arms fire we had been hearing grew louder and closer. German troops started firing on us from the houses on either side of us, which they now occupied. I told Oscar that it was time for us to withdraw to a safer position, but being new to action, he wanted to follow orders rigidly and stay.

The small arms fire aimed at us increased from the surrounding houses, in spite of us firing into the buildings with our Browning machine gun and firing a few H.E. shells. A Spandau, a German machine gun firing at a very high speed, easily identified by its barking sound, opened up on us from one of the buildings, and the German infantry started firing grenades from their rifles at our tank. They were getting closer and closer. Oscar still refused to go back so I told him in no uncertain terms on the intercom, so that Charlie and Eric would hear me, "Look Oscar, this is ridiculous, we have got to go back in the next few minutes, or we will get knocked out by a bazooka, if you want to stay, then you can do so, but when we go, we will take the tank with us."

He was still very hesitant and mumbled, "But we have been ordered to stay and got to stop any Jerry tanks from coming up this road."

Suddenly there was a sharp crack of a grenade exploding on the side of the tank, and Oscar got some of the blast of the grenade in his face, which completely numbed him. There was no time to lose now. I came up on the radio just saying, "A7C being fired at, coming back, over and out."

On the intercom I told Charlie to move back as fast as we could. The Squadron Leader came back immediately, "Sunray here, A7C watch out at the crossroad, I repeat watch out at the crossroads, there is a Jerry SP gun on your right, I repeat again, SP gun on your right, over and out."

I looked to my right as we turned left into the main road taking in at a glance the German SP gun, about 30 yards away on the left hand side of the road, with its vicious 88mm gun pointing directly at us, with a Churchill Flame Thrower immediately on the right hand corner, well alight.

For a moment the world stood still. Even now I can see this picture plain in my mind. Then everything erupted at the same moment. The turret of the Churchill lifted straight up in the air with a terrific roar, and came down next to the tank. The German SP gun fired at us at the same time, the armoured piercing shot passing inches in front of our tank. Charlie saw the tracer of the shell going past his nose, and never reacted more quickly in all his life. Within seconds our Sherman tank was in top gear racing down the road at a speed Sherman's were never built for. By the time the German loader had had time to put the second round into the breech of their gun, the aim of the gunner had been put out by the speed at which we were racing away from him, the shell going well past us. We pulled in next to the Squadron Leader, reported back and rejoined our troop. Oscar had recovered by now from the blast of the grenade, but was still very shaken up.

All the tanks were fairly closely clustered together on the side of the main road, facing in the direction from which we had just come. Our squadron consisted of three Cromwell tanks, with every fourth tank in each troop a Sherman Firefly. Parked right next to us was another Sherman with

118

only a crew of three, awaiting a new tank commander, as Bob, their commander, had just been injured and taken back to base.

Whilst we were brewing up at the back of our tank a truck arrived. Jimmy Hague got out with all his kit and loaded it on to the Sherman. He looked pale, apprehensive, and was shaking. He had been back at base awaiting transport home for the last few days under the Python return scheme, which applied to anyone who had completed five years front line service. As there was a shortage of transport he was still at the base when Bob was injured and had been asked to take over Bob's tank until another replacement could be found.

I gave him a sweet mug of tea to calm him down. He had barely finished loading his kit when the troop leader, Lieutenant Kirby came up and gave him some instructions, which he marked on his map.

Jimmy then climbed up into his tank and they started moving forward. They had moved forward only two feet when the tank lurched sideways and stopped because the tank had shed its track. It would take quite some time to repair the track, so Kirby told Oscar we would have to take its place.

We were told to move up the road and take the next turning. He showed me on the map, which I duly marked with a chinagraph pen, where to take up our position to engage some buildings occupied by German SS infantry, which were causing us a lot of trouble and who were holding up our advance. We pulled out at speed moving up to the new position between a barn and a farmhouse from where we could see the houses between hedges and copses across a field, which I had identified on the map. Everything was very still and quiet.

I had loaded the gun with an H.E. shell, gave Eric the OK over the intercom, and he fired. As I watched I saw the tracer of an A.P. shell coming back and passing straight over us, practically taking off the aerial. I immediately loaded an A.P. shot and shouted fire. I heard the firing pin click, but nothing happened. Eric pressed the trigger several more times. I reported miss-fire and told Charlie, "Reverse behind the building."

As we were moving back another A.P. shell came straight at us but went past our front, as we started moving.

We got our breath back in the shelter of the farmhouse and I waited the regulation five minutes before removing the dud shell, with tender care, from the breech of the gun. A farmer came out of the building, wondering what was going on and I passed him the shell, saying, "Put this very carefully into that ditch over there."

On reporting back to the troop leader we were ordered to return at full speed to rejoin the squadron, as A6C, Jimmy's tank, had just been knocked out by the SP gun, that had previously fired on us. All the crew in the turret were killed, including Jimmy, who had got so close to returning home for good. This was the sad end to Jimmy's war. He had been in action for five years. He should have returned home. Did he have an inkling that this was going to happen when I had last seen him only about half an hour ago and made him his last mug of tea?

We moved back the way we had come. The regiment was advancing down the main road. We passed Jimmy's smashed tank, which was still in the same position where it had shed its track. Past the still burning SP gun, which had been knocked out, with two bodies laying by its side. Past the crossroads with the burned-out Churchill Flame Thrower, which had no doubt saved our lives by exploding at the right time.

Albala had been the first of my friends to be killed at Villers Bocage shortly after the landing. Then Ralph Parker was injured at Ellon, near Jerusalem in Normandy, at the end of June and evacuated back to England. Then Jimmy Hague was killed at Shilberg, which was to be followed soon by Jimmy Gibson's death near Oosterhout in Holland.

I often wonder why I am still alive? If the gun barrel had not hit the tree and ruined the traversing gear we would have had to stay and battle it out with the two Tigers. We would have been well out-gunned and not stood a chance.

If the turret of the Churchill had not blown up just at the right moment, the SP gun could not have missed our tank.

If Jimmy's tank had not shed a track, we would have been in the exact position where Jimmy was killed.

If the gun had not misfired, something which had never happened before in either mine or my friends experience with a 17-pounder gun, we would not have reversed, and the second A.P. shot would have gone clean through the turret.

So many 'ifs'. Too many 'ifs'? Statistically I should have been dead, so who had been watching over me? Why? Was it in order that my children and grandchildren could be born? Destiny, what is destiny?

We moved on into Schilberg on the 19th January to meet up with the rest of the squadron. The Squadron Headquarter troop tanks and some Rifle Brigade troops had taken up position in a small square in the village. The Squadron Leader briefed us, addressing the Troop Leader, "I want you to move up the road and about five hundred yards ahead you will come to a crossroad. Take two tanks straight across taking up a position 100 yards ahead and send one tank each down to the left and right, also taking up positions 100 yards away from the crossroads. We have to guard against any counter attacks from the Jerries. Keep your heads down as you move up and watch out for snipers as there are still some Jerry infantry milling about in the houses on either side of the road but hopefully they will have dispersed by the morning. Each tank will report when you are in position, and of course you must keep on net all night."

We moved off slowly, only our heads sticking out of the tank. Oscar, the tank commander, was now watching again the houses on the right and I did the same on the left. As we approached the crossroad, the Troop Leader Lieutenant Kirby, came up on the B set, "A7C, take the turning on your left and report back to Sunray when you have taken up your position, over and out." I saw his Cromwell tank speeding up the road, followed by another, both driving quickly across the crossroad. Oscar now ordered Charlie to turn left and I watched the Cromwell behind us turning right, disappearing in the distance.

As we moved slowly along the road, Oscar was nervously looking for a suitable parking position at a bend on the right hand side to give us a better view of the road in front of us. We pulled in, asked Eric to stay on guard at his gun position and slid off the tank with our small arms, to make sure that there was no one about. Charlie got the primus out and put the kettle on whilst Oscar got back on the tank to report our position.

Suddenly I heard him shout down to me, "Oy, Buzz, come up here quick, I can't get through on this fucking set." I jumped up on to the tank and checked the radio. Everything looked all right, everything was still set as it had been, but I could not get any signals. It was as dead as a doornail. I could not understand it as it had only been minutes since the Troop leader had sent us a message. I went through all the prescribed checks again, without any luck.

I got off the tank and joined the others, "Sorry, boys, there is nothing I can do, the set is dead. We can't get a message through and we can't leave here with the tank. Someone will have to walk back and tell the Squadron Leader." They all agreed and quite unanimously pointed at me saying, "Buzz, you are the op. If you can't get the message through on the set you must get it through on foot. We will stay here on guard."

I gulped down a cup of tea and walked off, carrying my sten gun, being well aware that there were still Jerries moving about, walking quietly close in the shade of the buildings. As I was even more aware that the R.B.'s were very trigger-happy and would shoot at anything that moved before asking questions, I stepped into the middle of the road, into the full moonlight, when I was halfway towards our H.Q. position, whistling loudly 'It's a long way to Tipperary'. On approaching the tanks, I also started waving and shouting, and was let in by a couple of R.B.'s on guard.

I made my way through to the Squadron Leader, saluted him and reported that our 19 set had broken down. He said, "All right, leave your tank here, I will send up another tank"

"But Sir, my tank is still up there, guarding the approach road, I walked here," I replied.

"Bloody fool, don't you know that there are still Jerry infantry all over the place?"

I couldn't help but smile and replied, "Of course I know Sir, can't you see that this walk has taken ten bloody years off my life?"

He too started smiling, saying, "OK, I will send Sergeant Waters up with his tank. You go up with him and show him where your position is and then come back here with your Firefly and try and get your radio set sorted out pronto so that you are ready for action in the morning. Go on, off you go now."

I rode up on Sergeant Waters' tank and our crew were only too happy to see me, and return to S.H.Q.

After having had some supper, I had another look at our radio set, which was still quite dead. I suddenly had an inspiration. I jumped across into the tank commander's side and examined his headset and its connection to the mains. There it was, Oscar had twisted the triangular connector and shorted everything out, when he was nervously moving with his hands, when we had moved up. I unplugged it, re-connected it properly and lo and behold, the set sprang back to life.

The Advance

The briefing by the Squadron Leader was short, to the point and very unpleasant. My stomach turned into a solid ball. Charlie, our driver, used some of the foulest language possible, using innumerable four letter words. Eric, the gunner, muttered something not very complimentary under his breath. Stan, the tank commander, quite new to being in battle, was very keen and, with shining eyes, willing to go anywhere in his ignorance. I made up the fourth member of the crew, the wireless operator and loader of the guns, and second in command.

I shall never forget that day. Sunday the 18th of March 1945. We had only just rejoined the regiment in a brand new Firefly as our previous tank had been badly damaged in battle. We had just taken delivery of it, had sufficient time to load our gear, but had not had a chance to test and check out our new acquisition.

We were deep inside Germany, an impenetrable forest looming only a short distance ahead of us, black and uninviting, had held up the tank column. Three attempts had been made to get through the German defences, without much success, and with very heavy losses.

We, No 7 troop, had been chosen from A Squadron for one last attempt. We were told to try and get through before dusk. Only one infantry platoon was available to cover our flanks during the advance. The major, with his bristling moustache and carefully knotted desert scarf, was not very happy about sending us down the road either. So we cracked jokes, that weren't funny, and tried to appear as unconcerned as possible. I was as scared as always when I knew that battle was about to commence.

I nipped inside the tank, checked the wireless and made sure I was still 'on net' our lifeline to the regiment. We had used it to listen to the BBC all morning. I put one of the high-powered armour-piercing shells into the breechblock of the 17-pounder gun, and fed a new belt into the Browning machine gun. I loaded my Sten gun and put some grenades within easy reach round the top of the turret. Dusk was approaching fast, and we did not have much time left.

The troop leader started up and we followed like lambs being led to the slaughter. About eight infantrymen crouched on the back of our tank until we reached the wood. The trees suddenly started closing in on us. The infantry boys, all R.B. (Rifle Brigade) jumped off the tanks and formed up on either side. The undergrowth was so thick that they had to keep to the ditch at the side of the road. Passing two of our burnt-out tanks on the road did nothing to boost our morale.

The troop of four tanks, three Cromwell and our Firefly, moved along the road at walking pace. We sat on top of the tanks with feet inside the hatch, earphones clipped tightly to the head, with one ear uncovered, trying to listen to any unusual sounds over the din made by the tanks. We were sitting ducks. They could hear us coming for miles. We couldn't even see them.

As the tanks rumbled on the tension mounted. By now the infantry boys were crawling in the ditches. We slowed down still further, travelling with our very long gun pointing over to the right, eyes strained for any suspicious movement, any strange reflections. All I could see were trees and shrubs. Not a move anywhere.

Suddenly there was a blinding flash. I could just see a tree being cut in half in front of me. The blast threw me onto the turret floor of the tank before I could hear the bang. The earphones were still tightly on my spinning head.

I heard a voice coming through the crackle, "...being fired upon. Seven Charlie has been knocked out. Only one man bailed out. The rest of the crew must have bought it."

I recognised the voice of our troop leader. He was talking about us, using our code name. Well, I wasn't dead. I was still here. I looked to my right where Stan should have been. There was only an empty hatch through which I could see a dark sky now. Stan must have got out all right. That meant they got Eric and Charlie. Eric and Charlie, well, they were not going to get away with it.

I looked through the periscope and saw the stump of tree that had been cut in half right in front of me. That must be it, that's where the Jerries were. The Browning was right in front of me. I just squeezed the trigger and watched the bullets rip into the dense shrub.

Above the din I heard Eric's familiar voice, "Here, Buzz, what are you firing at?"

So they had not got him after all, "It's the Jerries," I shouted back, "go on, traverse the turret if you can, spray the bastards, go on, let them have it."

I happily carried on squeezing the trigger. I had not felt so happy for a long time. Now the other tanks joined in. Concentrated fire from all the tanks followed my tracer bullets. A beautiful sight. Nothing could survive that hail of bullets. I looked down into the driver's compartment and Charlie was grinning back at me.

I shouted over the intercom, "Is the tank alright?" and got a curt reply, "You bet it is."

I reported over the air to the troop leader that we were all right and fit for action. A shadow over the tank commander's hatch announced the arrival of a sheepish Stan who had been lying in a wet ditch for the last few minutes. The radio crackled into life and the troop was ordered to return to the squadron. We all pumped a few more belts into the shrub for good measure, collected our infantry boys, and moved at top speed back down from whence we came.

A young cockney had seen it all happen. He was full of it, "Cor, matey, you were dead lucky. I sor it all. One of them there bazookas 'it the tree in front of yer tank. I sor it being fired. Cor, you would have 'ad it, if it 'ad 'it yer. I fink you got 'im all right though matey. I wouldn't be in one of them there coffins fer anyfink."

I was pleased with myself, that was the appreciation we deserved. I settled back in the tank, as we were rumbling back along the road.

Suddenly I sat up with a jerk. The breechblock was wide open. I had only loaded our 17-pounder gun with one of our new, high-powered, armoured piercing shells before we started out, and now there was its empty shell case on the turret floor. I touched it and burned my hand. Impossible, we had not fired the big gun since we had taken delivery of the tank - or had we?

I looked across at Eric, nudging him and pointing to the empty shell case. He shouted across the din, "Keep quiet and get rid of that shell case as quick as you can and don't let anyone see it."

Suddenly it all clicked into place. We had not been fired on at all. We had fired our gun, the shell had hit the tree and cut it down, and the blast from the muzzle of our gun had blown me down into the turret. I then found out that when the tank had been delivered they had incorrectly connected the cables from the firing buttons. The Browning trigger had been connected to the big gun and the trigger for the big gun to the Browning. When Eric thought he had spotted some movement he wanted to fire a burst with the machine gun but the big gun went off instead.

That night an artillery barrage was laid onto the forest, which continued all through the night. The Royal Air Force supported it with a bombardment. A lot of noise, a beautiful sight, and an uneasy conscience.

Next morning, on Thursday the 19th, we moved in again. We drove down the road at full speed. In the light of the bright sunny morning the forest looked less foreboding. A quiet calm now hung over everything. There was not a soul in sight as the advance continued.

As we were driving along the dusty road I sat on the rim of the turret and saw a lone soldier, wearing a black beret, a shoulder bag and carrying a Sten gun in his right hand, walking up towards us. As we got nearer I realised that it was Teddy, who had been training with me at Farnborough and who had been in the Pioneer Corps with me before that.

I waved and yelled down to him, pointing forward, "Oy, Teddy, this is the way to the sharp end, you are going the wrong way."

He waved back as we passed him giving me a funny smile and just walked on. I forgot all about the incident until we met again after the war, and only found out then that I had deeply hurt him, as he was walking back from his tank, which had just been knocked out and both his driver and co-driver had been killed.

The Cavalry Charge

In a desolate field, somewhere in Germany, the Squadron Leader called us to a special conference in March 1945. It was about 3pm. The grass was still wet from the morning rain. The tanks were parked under the hedges for cover against air reconnaissance. We had been advancing for nearly a week, were tired and dirty, and had hoped that another squadron would relieve us as things had quietened down a little.

We sat under a clump of trees waiting to be briefed by the Squadron Leader. I instinctively knew this was going to be something big and sat with my crew watching the major approach us, with his clipboard under his arm, his scarf tucked into his greatcoat, as had been the fashion in the eighth army in North Africa. He was bare-headed and his black beret was tucked under the epaulette of his greatcoat.

He sat on a tree trunk and said, "As you will have guessed these dense black woods in front of us are milling with Jerries. It is essential for us to get through. The 5th Royal Tank Regiment tried earlier today losing three tanks. There is no way we can get through there in daylight. There is a tank barrier just before the village, which has not been closed yet by the Jerries, as they seem to be confident that no one can get through the woods. I have decided the only way through is a cavalry charge during the night, advancing at top speed with all guns blazing. 7 troop will be leading."

Yes, I thought, you bugger, we can lead and you follow on behind. I glanced at Charlie, our driver, sitting next to me, he turned up his eyes and said, "Sod this."

"You will move up the track you can see at the edge of the forest, it leads to the village about four miles away. You should make it in 12 to 15 minutes. The lead tank will be the troop leader, followed by 7 Charley with its long 17-pounder gun (with me in it) with the other two Cromwell tanks close behind. In the centre will be a half-track with a handful of infantry. You will be leaving at 1am. I will follow with the Squadron HQ troop 20 minutes later, and then the other troops will follow in 20 minute intervals, all advancing with guns blazing. You can now stand down, check the guns, grab some grub, draw a special ration of rum for each tank. Good luck boys, see you in Ahaus."

This had never been done before. We had cooked our meal of skinless sausages, beans and hard compo biscuits (as we had no fresh bread) behind the tank on a petrol fire in an old oil drum, which we always kept tied to the back of our tank. I now had my first swig of the rum, burning my throat as I tried to swallow it too quickly and felt instantly much better, getting quite excited about the prospect of doing something so different. The more rum I swigged, the better I felt.

I was on wireless watch for two hours and then I had a kip fully clothed under the back of the tank. At 00.45 the Troop Leader roused us. We climbed into our tank. Charlie started the engine, Stan the tank commander and myself stood on our seats, so that we were halfway out of the turret and could see much better and surrounded ourselves with grenades ready to drop over the side. I had my Sten gun in my hand. The headphones crackled and the troop leader came over loud and clear, "Able Seven go, go, go, follow me, over and out."

I could dimly see his tank move off and we followed as close behind as we could, with the other two Cromwells behind us, with the half-track in the middle.

After we had driven into the forest for only a short distance we could see German troops milling about and all the tanks opened up firing machine guns in both directions, with the infantry in the half track firing their small arms. I fired my Sten gun and dropped a few grenades as far as I could into the surrounding black forest. Eric fired a high explosive shell into a woodcutter's building at the side of the road, which went instantly up in flames. Stan shouted to me across the din, "Put another H.E. up the spout, that'll show the bastards"

I quickly reloaded the 17-pounder and climbed back up to fire my Sten gun and watch the surrounding inferno. I had my earphones on and the troop leader shouted excitedly over the air, "There is a German lorry coming down the lane towards me, I am going straight for it" The leading tank hit it full on, pushing it into the ditch with the ammunition on the lorry exploding like fireworks. A sea of flames, both sides of the lane, advanced like fury with us. A German lorry loaded with jerrycans of petrol then got in the way, was hit full on, and went up in flames illuminating our advance.

As Eric was firing the big gun again at a house to our right, amongst the trees, which also went up in flames, the long barrel hit a tree smashing the traversing gear and making the turret spin like a mad top. I had quite expected that, as it had happened to us once before and had my feet firmly on the seat.

The spinning turret soon came to rest as we drove on at full speed over humps and bumps, through the open gate of the tank barrier straight into the village. The tanks dispersed, one going forward, two turning and guarding a crossroad. We could not see any German troops to engage, so the infantry dismounted and started searching the houses. We guarded the road we had come from. We sweated manhandling the turret, turning it slowly, until Eric had lined up the crossbars of the telescope, on to the turning we had just come round, exactly 300 yards away. Should a German tank come round that corner, Eric had only a second to fire, and then bale out in case he missed.

Stan rushed up to me with a German soldier, who had just arrived on a bike and was holding on to it for dear life, guarded by one of the infantry, "Come on Buzz, find out what he knows"

The German was surprised I could speak his language. He had been sent down to order the German unit they thought was still in the village to close the tank barrier. He said,"I said goodbye to them when I left and told them I would probably not be able to get back, when I saw this wall of flames advancing towards us. I am glad I was right, because I am out of it now, and for me the war is over."

We sat anxiously in our tank waiting for a German Panther or Tiger to come round the corner and were concerned that we might fire at our own tanks. We need not have worried. Twenty minutes after our arrival we heard a lot of firing, tank engines revving at top speed and coming ever closer, again accompanied by a wall of flame, heralding the arrival of the HQ troop. The other two troops arrived in intervals with a similar furore.

As our traversing gear turning the turret with its 17-pounder gun was not working, we had no way of firing effectively at the enemy, with either the main gun or the machine gun. We moved along the village street to take cover further back and the Squadron Leader's tank took up our position, guarding the road on which we had just arrived.

This sleepy old German village had suddenly been disturbed. All the old-fashioned window shutters were closed in both houses and shops. Some of the civilians had fled but others had been hiding in the cellars and were routed out by the infantry, who also found a few German soldiers who surrendered only too willingly, looking forward to be sent to a POW camp.

As our tank was out of action now I went into one of the empty houses to enjoy the luxury of sitting on a real flush toilet. Normally, in action, you had to jump off the tank with a shovel with your ration of two sheets of toilet paper when there was a lull in the shelling. You ran to the nearest hedge, dug a hole and crouched down, hoping the

Jerries would not commence shelling until you had finished. If they did, your mates would look on and you would be wondering whether you would get a shell splinter up your arse. With all these exciting activities and having achieved our goal, we were on a high and getting lax.

A Royal Tiger managed to cut through the woods and came up on the road behind us. The gunner in the Squadron Leader's tank guarding this approach to the village was not quick enough to spot him. The Germans fired their powerful dreaded 88 mm gun. Both he, and Sid the Squadron wireless operator were killed instantly. Fred the driver and Jack, the co-driver, managed to bale out before their tank was hit a second time. The Royal Tiger then reversed and disappeared into the forest.

B Squadron advanced in exactly the same way we had. We warned them of the lurking Royal Tiger and they managed to knock it out.

As our tank was useless with its broken traversing gear we managed to get a replacement Firefly, with a 17-pounder, the following day.

Changing over tanks is very much like moving home. You get so attached to it, you know every nook and cranny, you know the sound of the engine and you hear and feel how the tracks move. You get to love it. It becomes part of you.

It was hard to get used to our replacement tank because it was so revolting. The last operator had been killed in the tank quite recently and no one had been given enough time to clean it up. My side of the turret and the cupola had deep shell splinter marks in it. My foldable seat had been soaked by the previous operator's blood, which had dried up in the upholstery and the stench of rotting flesh still permeated the air. The splinter marks on the side showed exactly how he had been killed. There, but for the grace of God, go I went through my head. I shivered with fear.

I never knew the guy who had died on my seat, but I could see him in my mind and formed a close bond with him. No doubt this was meant to be a lesson to me, having felt so exhilarated during the advance, I had to be reminded again that death was only around the corner.

***

The strange thing had always been that whenever we went into action. Through the briefing we were told that this action would be a pushove. That we were getting artillery and air support. I got very frightened and could not sleep properly the night before. But as soon as we went into battle with our artillery support guns firing incessantly and German shells and air bursts coming back, there was no way one could mistake these sounds, in spite of all the din being made, I started to relax.

Once in battle I wanted to stay there and wanted the action to go on for as long as possible, for I knew that when we pulled out for a rest, I would be more frightened the next time we went in. At the same time I loved coming back for the rest as we were often able to go to a forward shower unit, where we would be able to have the luxury of having a hot shower and get fresh, clean, warm clothing to wear afterwards.

Many things I will never forget

During the fighting we saw many dead cows and horses, often covered in flies, and I will never forget the peculiar sweet stench that filled the air before we could burn the bodies with vast quantities of petrol.

I will also never forget the body of a young German officer I saw with flies crawling in and out of his eyes, mouth and nose. He held a wallet in his right hand, which he must have pulled out of his pocket just before he died. His family photos where strewn around him, one of a pretty young woman holding a baby in her arms, and a very young girl with long blonde hair holding a little Welsh Terrier on a short lead.

I can still see the long column of German soldiers sitting and laying desolate at the side of a road, waiting to be sent back to a prisoner of war compound, with many wounded amongst them. I hopped down from the tank when we stopped and looked at a stretcher at the roadside, which had been pulled a little away from the rest of the soldiers, on which lay a man completely covered by a blanket. I heard him moan and groan and he must have heard me approach because he called out in German, "Kamerad, Kamerad, bitte erschieße mich, gib mir den Gnadenschuss," freely translated into, "Mate. Mate, please shoot me. Give me the coup de grace."

I pulled back the blanket and looked into his face, into his pleading eyes and saw the terrible deep wound in his stomach. I got out my pistol and he said again in German, looking straight at me, "Please, please shoot me."

My crew watched me and the German soldiers further down the road sat up and looked. I was just about to press the trigger, feeling in how much pain he must be, when I realised that I did not really know that he was going to die. No, I could not do it. I stood next to him, kneeled down so that he could hear me better and said in German, "Look mate, you are not going to die yet, there will be an M.O. here soon and hopefully he can help you and ease your pain."

The man still looked at me in despair, and repeated again and again, "Mate. Mate, please shoot me, please shoot me."

I felt terrible, but could not bring myself to shoot him. I climbed back up on the tank, jumped into my hatch and called up the Squadron Leader on the A set saying, "A7C to Sunray. There are a lot of German soldiers here with many wounded, some seriously, waiting to go back. Is there a chance to send up an M.O.?" and gave him the map reference of our position.

We got an immediate reply, "Will do what I can, in the meantime you must swan on and not allow yourself to be held up, follow the route given, over and out."

Nor will I ever forget when we had entered a small German village and were advancing slowly towards a barn with a few R.B. infantrymen at our side. The leading infantryman was carrying a Bren gun in his right arm, level with his hip, pointing it straight towards the barn door. Suddenly a small door, set into the barn door, opened and a smartly dressed German SS officer jumped out, looked at us and shouted, "Du Englisches Schwein, Heil Hitler" (You English pig, Heil Hitler), raising his arm in the Nazi salute and then trying to pull the pistol out of the leather holster, strapped to his belt. As he fumbled with it the soldier with the Bren gun, standing only a few feet in front of him, pressed the trigger and fired a burst, cutting the German in half, with blood spurting all over the place

"Serves him f…ing right. Fancy the stupid bastard, trying to draw a pistol on me."

When seeing the dead corpses of men in the fields and knocked out tanks, I always thought of the poem by a Russian soldier *Wait for me and I'll return"* and also this poem by A.E. Houseman: -

Here dead lie we,

Because we did not choose

To live and shame the world from which we sprang,

Life to be sure is nothing much to lose,

But young men think it is,

And we were young.

These poems helped me to get through the war emotionally.

Major Dr Rudie Walter

The 1st Royal Tank Regiment of the 7th Armoured Division had accepted the surrender of Hamburg on 3rd of May 1945 occupied it for two days and moved into Schleswig Holstein on the 5th May when the German army surrendered in North West Germany.

The regiment was now in the village of Meldorf, surrounded by thousands of German troops ambling about, wondering what was going to happen to them now that the war had finished.

Russell, another trooper in the squadron, and me were the only German speakers in the regiment. We had been ordered to walk about amongst the German prisoners of war, inspecting their identity papers and sorting out the SS from the ordinary military personnel as they had to be put into separate compounds.

I was back at my tank when a smartly dressed, round-faced German major approached me, clicked his heels, saluted and asked in German, "I hear you speak fluent German. May I talk to you?"

"Yes, by all means, what can I do for you?"

"Let me introduce myself first. I am Major Dr. Rudolf Walter. I am an eye specialist at the German army eye hospital in the fields across the road from here. If you would be kind enough to read this letter that I have removed from my commanding officer's file without his knowledge you will understand my position better."

That is how I first met Rudie on the 10th May 1945.

The letter was from the Gestapo Headquarters in Berlin and addressed to Colonel X, Commanding Officer of the German Army Eye Hospital, in the field at the Eastern Front. It was short and to the point and read, "Under no circumstances may Major Dr. R. Walter be promoted beyond the rank of Major as he is politically unreliable."

An SS General had signed the letter with a flourish. I looked up in great surprise, "Tell me, why did the Gestapo consider you to be politically unreliable?"

"It's a long story, is it OK to tell you now?"

I told him to sit down. We were just making some tea behind the tank. I offered him a tin mug and took one myself. When I offered him some English cigarettes his face lit up, "I have not smoked a decent cigarette for years."

Sherman tank at work (from Bovington archives)

143

Eric Marsland (left) with captured Nazi flag, Schleswig Holstein

I gave him the whole pack and we settled down while he told me his story.

He had been a well-known eye specialist in West Berlin. His tutor and mentor had been the famous and sought after Berlin eye specialist Dr. William Luftig, who had a flourishing private practice. He was the founder and specialist in curing defective vision by treatment, using exercises, massages and heat treatment, so that patients did not have to wear glasses. Dr. Luftig was Jewish and had married Rudie's sister Käthe in 1925.

When Hitler came to power, mixed marriages were frowned upon in Nazi Germany. Dr. Luftig and Käthe were quite wealthy and decided to emigrate to England in 1933, at a time, when they were still able to take their money with them. They left the practice and their large apartment in the West End of Berlin to Rudie asking him to look after Dr. Luftig's elderly mother, who lived nearby.

144

After the Kristallnacht on the 9th November 1938 when the Nazis burned down synagogues in Germany and arrested most male Jews sending them to concentration camps Rudie decided that it was not safe for Dr. William Luftig's mother to live on her own. He suspected even then that all Jews would be sent to camps and exterminated. He quietly moved her into his apartment late one evening so that she would not be seen by any of the other tenants. He did not register her with the police, as was required by all Germans, and therefore got no ration cards for her. He bought additional food on the black market. As far as the authorities were concerned she had just disappeared.

Initially, when he was called up into the army he was in an army eye hospital stationed in Berlin. The old lady died in 1942 and Rudie was faced with having to arrange a funeral for a woman who had no papers and did not officially exist. Fortunately one of his patients was a funeral director.

He went to see him and said, "Look here, Franz. We have known each other for a long time and I have helped you a lot with your eyes, as had my brother-in-law Dr. William Luftig before he left Berlin. Now I would like you to do me a favour. I have been hiding Dr. Luftig's mother in my flat. The old lady died on me last night."

"I thought there was someone else in the flat with you. When I last came for my treatment I heard some noises and you appeared a little distracted. I actually thought you had a new girlfriend staying with you, and wanted to keep it quiet," replied Franz. He continued, "It's not easy and the Nazis are spying on everything we are doing. It is going to be expensive as I will have to bribe some of my people and will have to pay a cash lump sum to the director at the cemetery."

"That's fine by me, you know I am not stingy. I leave it to you and the sooner you can arrange the funeral the better."

That's how Rudie managed to achieve, with great difficulties, bribery and corruption, to bury a person who did not exist.

The Luftigs had first set up a practice in London where Doctor Luftig was internationally known. Patients visited him from as far afield as New Zealand, Australia and Canada. Dr. Luftig also travelled with Käthe extensively from England to the United States, Canada and India making contact with other eye specialists in his field. Eventually they settled down in Hove near Brighton, buying a large house there in 1940.

Having finished his story Rudie asked me, "Would you please be kind enough and help me. Could you get in touch with my sister and brother-in-law as I am unable to do so as a prisoner of war. Tell them that I am still alive and OK. Also please tell them that unfortunately Dr. Luftig's mother passed away but died a natural and peaceful death being comfortable to the end. The apartment and practice in Berlin are still alright, although there has been some limited bomb damage."

I was very impressed by Rudie. He had saved the life of a Jewish woman in Berlin by hiding and feeding her. He had to bury her without documents when she died. He had risked his life to do all that. I could only agree to help him as best I could. I gave him a few packets of cigarettes, which were like gold dust at that time and which he gratefully accepted. Then I gave him a pat on the shoulder, advising him to safeguard the letter from Gestapo Headquarters to his Commanding Officer and produce it when he was interrogated as it would no doubt help him to get an early release from the P.o.W. camp.

Before being transferred from the R.T.R. to the Military Police as an interpreter and attached to the 245 Company Military Police in September 1945 in Berlin I was given two weeks leave to go home to England in June. I soon found Luftig's address and phone number in the Brighton telephone directory. They lived in Preston Park Road in Hove. When I phoned them to tell them that I had met Rudie and had news from him, they insisted that I should come and see them.

I arrived at their large and very impressive house and knocked on the wide front door. Käthe opened the door, embraced me and ushered me into their huge lounge full of oriental paintings, several man-sized brass Buddha and an immense oriental fireplace. The embossed ceiling was about twelve feet high. Dr. Luftig came running down the stairs and we sat around a small-engraved brass table in very comfortable armchairs. I had to tell them all about my meeting with Rudie. They were delighted to hear that he was alive but very concerned for him when they found out that he had sheltered Dr. Luftig's mother. They asked question after question but, of course, my knowledge was limited as I had only been with him for a short time.

I could describe the German military eye hospital to them in which Rudie still worked and tended to his patients where he had to make do with very limited equipment and shortages of hospital supplies.

Dr. Luftig then proudly showed me his two consulting rooms on the first floor of his house, with all the various instruments and heat lamps. He explained their functions to me in lay terms. He examined my eyes and assured me, that if I had time to spend a few months with him in Brighton he would be able to improve my eyesight so much that I would not need to wear glasses.

They were both strict vegetarians, living mainly on fruit and nuts but in spite of that they cooked me a delicious meal of toast, bacon and egg, which was served in the dining room.

After lunch we walked round their beautiful well-kept large garden. I chain-smoked, in spite of noticing that they did not smoke. As we became very good friends over the years I was only told much later, that they had to open all the windows in the house for days after I had left to get rid of the smell of the cigarette smoke and the bacon.

When I returned from my leave to Germany I was amongst the first British troops to be sent to Berlin then divided into four zones; American, Russian, French, and British. The city was in ruins.

Knocked out tanks were still littering the streets. In the Kaiserdamm, a main road leading straight up north from the Brandenburg Gate, which was the border between the Russian and British Zone. A German Royal Tiger tank had been dug in up to the hull into the tarmac with its 88mm gun pointing north in the direction from which the Russians had been advancing towards the Reichs Chancellery, where Hitler was desperately still trying to win the war. It had been knocked out by three shots placed closely together piercing the gun mantelet at its thickest part. I had never seen armour pierced like that by any of our guns and gained great respect for the rough looking, but obviously very effective Russian fighting machines.

At first we were stationed in the Berlin Olympic Stadium where we all ate in a large canteen. Outside the canteen were big dustbins into which we emptied our mess tins after eating. The German population was starving and they had not had any rations for a considerable time. Queues formed at the waste bins and as we scraped our leavings into them, the German civilians, some very old, some very young, scraped out the dustbins and fought over our leavings.

The 245 Company Military Police I was attached to soon moved into quarters in the Knesebeck Straße, just off the Kufürstendamm which is a major dual carriage road, running north to south from Charlottenburg to Wilmersdorf, up to the badly bombed out Gedächtnis Kirche, a large church. The ruin still stands to this day in its square, as a memorial to the war.

One day in October, I was walking up on the right hand side of the tree-lined Kurfürstendamm, with a tram rattling down on its track in the centre of the road, fenced off by railings when I heard a shout in English, "Hey, Mr. Ward, Mr. Ward, wait, wait."

It was Rudie, who was running across the road towards me, leaping across the railings, coming to a halt in front of me, panting. When he got his breath back he told me that he had been released very quickly and was back in his nearby apartment, where he had started up again as an eye specialist. He had heard from his sister that I had kept my promise and had been to see them, thanking me profusely. He insisted that I come to his home, where he showed me the repairs he had already carried out to the bomb damage. He had completely re-fitted the consulting room.

We became very friendly and one day he told me his most amazing story, "I was transferred from my post in Berlin to a specialist eye hospital on the Eastern front in the summer of 1944 to replace the second in command who had just been killed in action. Conditions were appalling. We were in an ankle-deep muddy field, not far behind the lines. We could hear the guns rumbling in the distance in the East. We were understaffed and casualties were pouring in. I was operating and tending to the wounded. We had been given strict orders to tend to the lightly injured first, so that they could be returned to the front as soon as possible, and not to waste time on the terminally ill.

As the Russians advanced in sharp spurts, the hospital was moved west towards Germany. As we were dealing with soldiers who had been wounded in their eyes and needed immediate attention, we had to remain reasonably close to the front line, which necessitated frequent moves, causing a lot of upheaval to our patients. During the very cold winter of 1944 the Russians advanced very fast and we had to move the hospital large distances. The winter was so cold that we had to wear thick gloves whilst operating which made life very difficult for us. Naturally we lost a lot of patients. By the end of March 1945 the Russians again advanced rapidly north and south of us. It was still very cold, the ground was frozen and covered in hard white snow and the Russian troops advanced towards us. I had known for a long time that we had lost the war, that this would be the end of the Nazis and that at last we would be free. However, I did not want to be taken prisoner by the Russians, as they understandably did not treat German prisoners very well, especially the officers. I also knew if I deserted to get to the West there was the danger that I would be picked up by an SS patrol and summarily executed.

I sat up late into the night pondering what I could do to get towards the western front so that I would be taken prisoner by the British instead of the Russians. Suddenly an idea hit me. Why not move the whole army hospital towards the West?

No sooner said than done. I sneaked into the office tent at 2 o'clock in the morning and forged a moving order on a typewriter, for our army eye hospital to be transferred to the outskirts of Hamburg. I signed it with a forged signature and rushed in to my colonel, telling him excitedly that we must move to Hamburg immediately.

My Commanding Officer looked at the order, then he looked at me with a twinkle in his eyes, "Major Walter, these orders look as though they have been written on our typewriter. Well done, you have got your orders now, so execute them at once. You are in charge of the move. It is your responsibility to get the hospital to Hamburg as quickly as possible without any losses. No one must be left behind, get moving."

I saluted smartly, rushed out to organise the move. It took some time to requisition a train that was returning from the front. In early April, during a heavy snowfall, we loaded all the patients and our equipment onto goods wagons. I had been able to organise a 1st class coach for the officers. We could hear the Russian guns thundering ever nearer as we started to depart, moving to the West.

It was a very slow journey going towards Berlin, with many stops and many delays. We had to go into sidings to allow troop trains with fresh troops to pass us going east. On one occasion we were strafed by a Russian fighter and ended up with more casualties in the goods wagons. But we kept moving slowly West. Just outside Berlin, in mid-April in a siding, we were strafed again and our engine was hit and exploded. There was a train with just two coaches and an engine parked on another siding. I went across to the stationmaster and told him that we had orders to move our army hospital to Hamburg and that we needed the engine with the driver, as ours had been killed. He said, "You can't have that engine, the train has been reserved for Dr. Göbbels and his family, in case they have to be evacuated."

I just pulled out my pistol and said, "Look, I have got movement orders; I have sick and wounded soldiers on my train. I have got to get them to Hamburg quickly before some of them die. They are badly needed to fight on in this war to defend Germany. Göbbels can make his own arrangements if he wants to get away with his family. You either get the engine fixed onto our train right now with the driver, or I will have you summarily executed here on the spot, for obstructing the army and sabotaging the war effort."

The engine, plus the two coaches, were very quickly joined to the front of our train. We rolled off slowly, but we officers were now travelling in comfort in the two additional luxury coaches. And so we moved on towards Meldorf, on the outskirts of Hamburg, where we arrived at the end of April, only shortly before the 3rd May, when Hamburg surrendered to British troops without a fight. The whole of the German army in Northwest Germany then surrendered on May 5th."

Within a day or so he said, "There is something else I must tell you now. When we were at the army hospital near Meldorf, you went around the officers and men and looked at their army papers. Do you remember a medium-height officer with glasses, an eye patch on his left eye and a slight stoop? He had papers stating that he was a Major in the parachute regiment."

"Sure, I remember him, he had a strange look about him and seemed ill at ease"

"I can tell you now that he was Heinrich Himmler."

"Well, why on earth did you not tell me that at the time, I certainly did not recognise him and I would have loved to arrest the chief of the SS, the murderer of millions of people."

"I actually wanted to do just that. I arranged a meeting with the other officers and suggested that we should arrest Himmler and hand him over to the British soldier with the red lanyard, who spoke fluent German. It would show that we German army officers had nothing to do with the Nazis and it would stand us in good stead with the British in the future. Some of the other officers did not agree. They were frightened that if this was done their names might be blacklisted by fervent Nazi supporters who may go underground to carry on the fight. They felt that they would not only endanger themselves but also their families. In the end they decided; if the British want Himmler, he is right here, they can arrest him themselves, we will not stand in their way and we certainly will not help him."

Rudie was one of the first Germans to come to England in a German car after the war to visit Dr. Luftig and his sister Käthe. We remained friends until he passed away in the 1960s, about five years after Dr Luftig had died a tragic death, falling over the bannister from the first floor of his house. I continued seeing his sister Käthe until she died in 1998 at the ripe old age of 93.

Life in Berlin 1945 - 1947

I was promoted to Squadron Quarter Master Sergeant (SQMS) as senior interpreter attached to the Military Police and subsequently the 89th Section of the Special Investigation Branch (SIB), dealing with crimes committed by British Military personnel and crimes committed by German civilians against British property.

Berlin was a defeated city and the four occupying powers divided Berlin into four separate sectors, the Russian, American, French and British sector. The Military Police of the four nations co-operated closely together. Vienna, in Austria, was in the same position, but in that city co-operation was even closer than in Berlin and jeeps containing one military policeman from each of the four powers patrolled the city streets. This was not done in Berlin, but we could always get immediate help from either the Russian or American patrols, when needed.

The Russian Military Police came under the jurisdiction of the Russian Kommandantura. As the Russians tended to speak more German than English I communicated with the Kommandantura frequently on behalf of the Military Police.

On one of the occasions there I suggested off the cuff to the duty officer, a captain, that it would be a good idea to organize a football match between the two military police forces at the Berlin Olympic Stadium, which was in the British sector. He jumped at the idea, saying it was a great idea, that they would love but unfortunately he could not authorise a game, but suggested I went with him, and he would ask his superior officer.

We went along a long corridor and came to an office in which sat his colonel. The colonel welcomed me and he and the captain chatted away in Russian. The colonel then picked up the phone, talked for a while in clipped tones and I was told that they would have to see someone higher up. The captain took me up to the next floor to a large office guarded by a heavily armed soldier. I now quietly wondered whether I had perhaps over-stepped the mark. Anyway, I was ushered into this sumptuous office with a thick carpet, panelled walls covered in oil paintings and a huge desk. A very high ranking officer about 6'3" tall, covered in medals and red ribbons, rose from behind his desk, towering over me, shaking me by the hand so fiercely, that I thought he was squashing it.

He had obviously been briefed, as he spoke to me in German, ushering me over to a table laden with crystal carafes and glasses. He told me to take a seat and have a drink with him, as he was so pleased to meet a British soldier. He poured the neat vodka, adding only very little water, saying, "Come on, let's drink to us. The war is over and we have at last defeated the Nazi machine. Plenty of cause to celebrate."

We clinked glasses and I had to empty my glass in one gulp, as was the custom, which also meant that the glass was immediately refilled. After the third glass he leant back in his chair and said, "So your football team wants to play ours?"

"Well" I replied, "yes, but this is only a suggestion and it would be great fun for the two teams to play now at the Berlin stadium where the Olympic games were held under Hitler in 1936."

He smiled, "How good is your team?"

"We are just ordinary soldiers, none of us have ever been professional football players. We just enjoy the fun of the game."

He smiled even more, pouring me another drink, "Look, quite confidentially, I can't agree to a game being played until I have seen how good your team is. Just imagine if our team would lose? Some of those bloody Germans will be watching, and it would never do for us to be seen to be beaten by a British team."

I finished my drink and thanked him for his hospitality. After a lot of backslapping, he once more gripped my hand in his huge palm. He never came to see us play and we never managed to get to play the Russian team.

Eventually I became very friendly with one of the Russian interpreters called Pavlov. He was a private soldier. I soon noticed that during discussions we were interpreting, he sometimes replied direct, making important decisions without referring to his superior officers. As very senior Russian officers also treated him with a certain amount of deference, it became obvious to me that he was an important political commissar. I invited him over to my private quarters at the Military Police Headquarters in the Kaiserdamm, which had previously been the German Central Police

Station with large garages and an abundance of prison cells and he came to visit me many times.

I had a nicely furnished sitting room and a bedroom. Pavlov loved the same classical music as myself and we played Beethoven and Tchaikovsky, whilst playing chess, drinking vodka and eating to our hearts content. Apart from speaking excellent German, he spoke fluent English and French. He was very well read including Dickens and Shakespeare. We had many interesting discussions, but I soon learned that I had to keep off politics. As soon as a political issue arose his mind became a blank, as though a curtain had dropped down in front of his eyes, and he just reiterated all the communist phrases.

One day towards the end of 1945 we were called out to a shooting in a bar, not far from our headquarters. I got into a jeep with two Red Caps. The two Military Policemen wore white belts with pistols in their holders, and their peaked red cap. I still wore my black beret from my Royal Tank Regiment. I had a pistol on my belt, but also carried a German Luger in a shoulder holster inside my battledress. We arrived outside the bar, which had a crowd of people standing around. We could hear the shooting and smashing of glass going on inside.

We carefully opened a side door and peeped inside. Two Russian officers, a major and a captain, were standing by a table and shooting at bottles behind the bar, with the barman ducked down behind it. I slowly walked towards them, followed by the two M.Ps. The major turned, saw me, put his gun back in to the pouch in his belt, walked towards me, opening his arms saying, "Towaritch,

Russian soldier Russian Kommandantura Berlin 1946

Towaritch" (Friend) and embraced me. He was obviously very drunk.

I also said, "Towaritch."

He went to a table, swept all the glasses off and got some more glasses from the bar, ready for us to have a drinking session. He then said something in Russian, which I did not understand.

I said: "Da, da" (Yes) so he embraced and kissed me. He said something again in Russian and I replied with, "Da, da" and he again embraced and kissed me. I felt we were doing all right, until after the fourth time, when instead of embracing and kissing me he hit me straight in the eye and his hand went down to his pistol pouch.

For quickness I got my Luger out before he managed to open his pouch, my safety catch clicked off with a loud click in the sudden deathly silence. The major looked straight down into the barrel of my Luger, raised his hands instantly and sat down in a chair, with his hands on the table in front of him. One of the M.Ps. called up the Russian patrol on the radio. To my relief two Russian M.Ps arrived within 10 minutes and strolled slowly into the bar.

I now pocketed my Luger. They did not speak any German, looked at me questioningly. I pointed at my eye and then at the Russian major and his pistol. The M.P. went up to the major and said something, whereupon the major got up and kicked him on the shin. The two policemen then set upon him, laying him across the table and beating him up. They dragged both the captain and the major into their jeep. We followed them in ours leaving the Germans to clear up the mess.

On arrival at the Kommandantura the two officers were marched into the large duty office. The smaller of the two policemen, who had been kicked on the shin, suddenly started to limp very badly and addressed the duty officer, pointing at his leg, at the major and my eye, which had swollen by now. The duty officer was only a lieutenant but he got up, grabbed the major with both hands and started beating him up, tearing off his epaulettes and throwing them on the floor. The major sat down, started to cry, pulled his medals off his chest and also threw them on the floor.

The duty officer apologised to me and said, "The major will be sent back to Russia and will be severely punished for attacking a British ally."

Life in Berlin was a lot of fun. We were the victors and behaved accordingly. In September 1945 I was invited to a party in the private flat of Paul Kerl, the German Police Chief of Charlottenburg where I first met Hildegard who eventually became my wife. He had been an inmate in a concentration camp but had survived. As he had been a former policeman, he had been appointed to this high position.

Hildegard impressed me, as she was different from the other German girls I had met. They had all been very subservient and fawning on me, she however was quite cheeky and independent. The party went on into the early hours of the morning and I walked her home, which was not far. She invited me up to her flat on the fourth floor, woke up her mother, introduced me to her by saying, "Look, look I found an English soldier who can speak German."

The mother made us a cup of what was supposed to be coffee, a rarity at that time in Berlin, and we chatted for a while. As it was very late by now, she asked me if I would like to stay the night, as it was now too late and it is easier to go back to my quarters in the morning. I agreed and she quickly made a bed up for me on the settee in the lounge. As I was about to settle down, Hildegard, before leaving the room, got my belt and pistol, which I had left on a chair telling me to put them under my pillow, as I was one of the victors and they the vanquished. We made arrangements to meet again when I left the following morning.

A few days later I saw Paul Kerl, the German Police Chief of Charlottenburg again about a minor incident, and he asked me if I'd like to go with him into the Russian Zone, the area surrounding the city of Berlin, saying we could go in his chauffeur-driven official Mercedes car. He had access to the Russian Zone, and wanted to get some vegetables, potatoes and drink, which we couldn't get here. He knew that the allied personnel couldn't go into the Russian Zone, but I would be OK with him.

Great, I replied, saying I'd love to go into the Russian Zone and have a look around, and if we can get some spare potatoes, no doubt Hildegard and her family would be delighted.

We left the following morning in his large drophead coupe, with the top open. Paul had a small banner of Charlottenburg fluttering from each of the two flags on the wings of his green car. The driver and co-driver were both in police uniform and Paul wore a smart police coat and had plenty of silver braid on his cap. I wore my white belt and pistol and looked very official. We both lounged comfortably in the back seats, and so we drove off. As we drove through the Russian sector of Berlin, the Russian Military Police waved us along. As we crossed into the Russian Zone we were passed quickly through the Zone barrier and were saluted by the many attractive and smart female Military Police. We sped along the roads away from the city, into the deep green countryside in beautiful warm sunshine. I felt I was on holiday, but was a little apprehensive and wondering whether we would get back into Berlin as easily as we had got out.

Soon I spotted a large, lonely farm in the distance, well off the road, with a narrow lane leading down to it. Paul said to the chauffeur, "That's Schmitt's farm, the place we are going to.

Slow down, drive along this muddy lane on the right and pull up in front of the farm house."

As we slithered down the lane Paul told me, that Schmitt had been in the concentration camp in Oranienburg with him, for holding back farm produce from the Nazis and supplying Berlin restaurants with black market food. His farm was confiscated, his family was evicted and the whole property was given to the local Nazi who had reported him. The Russians freed us and Schmitt was given his farm back. He found his wife and children, who had been forced to work as slave labour on another farm. The Russians took care of the Nazi informer and Schmitt has been appointed District farm Supervisor. He and Paul were great friends and he will make us very welcome.

As we pulled up outside the farm building, three noisy German shepherd dogs surrounded us and we waited for the farmer to come out and call off the dogs. As soon as Schmitt had locked the dogs in a shed he came and warmly shook Paul's hand. Paul introduced me, and Schmitt said he had never met a British soldier before, that he was so pleased to meet me, especially as I spoke such excellent German. We were invited inside to have a drink.

The farmhouse door led straight into a very large kitchen/sitting room, with a clean red tiled floor. A huge log fire was burning in the grate and a black steaming kettle was hanging from a chain by the fire. In one corner of the room was a solid fuel cooker, with various pots and pans sizzling away and a youngish woman in her mid-thirties, busying herself in front of it. She joined us at the long, highly polished wooden table in the centre of the room, surrounded by leather upholstered upright chairs.

I sat down on one of the chairs with my back to the fire. That was very welcome on this September day as the room was much cooler than the warm sunshine outside. I threw a carton of 200 English cigarettes into the centre of the table, to the whoops of delight from Herr Schmitt, who had not seen an English cigarette for years. He introduced me to his charming wife Inge and we all lit up cigarettes, deeply enjoying them. Inge then poured some boiling water into a metal coffee pot and in no time we all had a plate of hot sausages, bacon and fresh brown bread in front of us, helping ourselves to the delicious looking home made butter. Inge got out some small glasses and a bottle of strong plum brandy from a cupboard and we settled down to a feast.

They wanted to know so much about England, about me, and why I spoke such fluent German. Their two young boys joined us, stared at my uniform and then jumped about for joy, when I gave them a bar of Cadbury milk chocolate each, and some sweets. Herr Schmitt and Inge had suffered a lot under the Nazis but now that he had been re-instated in his farm and had managed to catch up with some of the work, which had been badly neglected, he was looking forward to a new future. He had been very lucky that no serious damage had been done to his farm buildings during the fighting.

Paul thanked Hans Schmitt for his hospitality and asked if he could let him have some vegetables, a sack of potatoes and also some for the driver and for the German girl friend of my English comrade Kenneth.

I added that I'd be delighted if he could spare some butter and fresh ham, saying I would get him another carton of 200 cigarettes from the car.

We soon loaded up, said our farewells and started on our homeward journey through the Russian Zone, arriving at dusk back in the Russian Sector, again being waved on and saluted by the Russian guards.

We had to stop to let a contingent of hundreds of Russian soldiers, six abreast, marching smartly down the road led by three banner-carrying soldiers with a band of drums and brass, singing at the top of their voices one of their national songs. It was like listening to a professional choir and brought tears to my eyes. Yes, the war was over, we had won and we were allies.

Paul dropped me with the sack of potatoes and goodies outside Hildegard's house. I took them up and gave these rarities to her mother, who did not believe her eyes when she saw the ham and butter. She could not thank me enough so I said, "Do me a favour, I love potato salad, please make some and I will come over tomorrow evening."

When I was on duty in our Military Police HQ in the Kaiserdamm during the following week, a well-dressed German couple came in with a beautiful Welsh terrier, who playfully jumped up at me, They wondered if I would be willing to look after the dog. A thoroughbred Welsh dog, and they had all her papers here. They loved her very much, but did not have enough food to feed her. It was breaking their hearts to give her away, but they knew I would be able to look after her so much better than they could. They called her 'Quicky' because she ran so fast, but her full name on her pedigree is 'Dida von Atrium'."

Whilst talking to me, Quicky started licking my hand, as though she knew what was being discussed. They had even brought her food dish with them. I had always wanted a dog, took instantly to Quicky, feeling very sorry for the couple having to give up their dog, but there just wasn't enough food available in Berlin, at that time, for the civilian population. Quicky stayed with me quite happily, although during the first few days she missed her old masters. I made her sleep in my bedroom at the foot end of my bed, and she obediently stayed there until I was asleep. But then she slowly crept up under my blanket and when I awoke in the mornings, she was always asleep next to me on my pillow.

In early 1946 I was transferred to the 89th Section of the Special Investigation Branch (SIB), who were billeted in a very large and beautiful villa at 11, Rüstern Allee in Berlin-Charlottenburg. Work there was much more interesting, as we dealt with serious criminal cases. All the personnel, except Sgt. Fitzjohn, called Fitz for short, who was also an interpreter, and myself, were ex-policemen. We dealt with several murder cases, a rape case and numerous break-ins into British property. A British court in Berlin dealt with some of the cases and I had to give evidence, presenting my reports, which I had usually typed out myself.

One day Lt. Dougie Lightwood, our commanding officer called me in and said, "Ken, I have got here a post-mortem report on a girl who was shot by a British soldier. It has been written by a German doctor at a local hospital. Can you translate it into English for me please. You realise, of course, how important it is that we know exactly every detail of the case. I need it as soon as possible, in fact, yesterday."

I took the report down to my desk and realised when I started reading, that I did not understand it. I phoned the doctor who had issued it at his hospital, and made an appointment to see him. I took the report with me, told him I needed to translate it into English, that I was bi-lingual, but that I could not understand the report fully, as I had no medical knowledge. We went through the report together and he explained to me in great detail, in lay terms, what it meant. I supplied him with plenty of cigarettes to keep him happy, making frantic notes, hoping I would remember everything. Of course I did not know the medical terms in German, nor did I know them in English. I soon realised that a lot of the medical words used were Latin which I could also use in English. However, I was still left in the end with a lot of words I could not find in my dictionary and decided to Latinise them by putting an 'a' or an 'o' at the end and just leaving them in. Needless to say, some of the sentences did not make much sense to me. My superiors and colleagues, all nodding their heads wisely and grunting at different intervals, read the report with great interest. It was duly submitted at court and neither the judge nor the counsel asked any questions.

About six months after the case finished we had a party at our mess. We had invited medical officers from the 84th Army Hospital, stationed in Berlin. We discussed one or two interesting cases with them, including the one with my translation of the post mortem report. The Captain reading through my report grinned at me never saying a word and no doubt was the only person realising what I had done.

We had a lot of fun working in the SIB section; we worked hard and played hard. One day in 1946 we were all invited to a party at the Military Police HQ. I drew the short straw and had to stay in the quarters to man the office. I was sitting comfortably in the large office on the ground floor, when the telephone rang in Dougie's office on the first floor. I raced up the wide winding staircase to his office, and as I was about to lift off the receiver, the phone stopped ringing.

Blast, I said to myself, staring at the phone, this might have been an important call. The phone started ringing shrilly downstairs and as I got to the bottom of the stairs it stopped.

Damn! I said out loud to no one in particular, when the upstairs phone started ringing. I ran up like a hare, but again the phone stopped ringing as I reached the office door. I was quite out of breath by now, when the main office phone downstairs started ringing again imperiously. This time I was lucky when I reached the phone, and Dougie said impatiently, "I have been trying to ring you for the

89 SIB Section Military Police Berlin 1947
Ken front row 2nd right Lt Dougie Lightwood 2nd left

last 20 minutes and have not been able to get an answer, what have you been doing?"

"The phone has also been ringing in your office..."

"Never mind your excuses, I haven't got time to discuss this now, we have got an important incident. You have got to act immediately. A dead Russian soldier has been found in Spandau, near the Russian border. There is no need for you to report this to the Assistant Provost Marshall (APM), he is here with me and knows what we are doing. Now this is what I want you to do. In the back of the basement garage is a big towing rope. Find it and take it up to the ground floor, leave it outside the garage where we keep the 15 cwt. truck and ring me back"

"Yes, sir, OK sir," I rasped, still out of breath and getting quite worried.

I ran down the steps into the basement, found the heavy towrope, took it up and dropped it outside the garage door. Then I ran back into the office and tried to ring the Military Police HQ number. Engaged. Tried again, engaged.

After about ten minutes I managed to get through and said, "Can I speak to Lt. Lightwood please?"

"Who?" came the reply.

"Lt. Lightwood from the 89 SIB."

"I don't know anybody by that name."

"Look," I shouted now, "Put me through to Lt. Lightwood straight away, this is an emergency. I know he is there, he just spoke to me, go and find him pronto."

After a while Dougie's voice came on, "What took you so long Ken, this is serious, did you find the rope?"

"Yes, Sir, I did."

"Good, well done, now this is what I want you to do. Put the rope in the truck, drive up to Spandau, you know where the Spandau prison is. Drive up to the main gate and take the road leading from there to the Russian sector. About half a mile from the border, you should find the body of a Russian soldier on the grass verge on the right hand side. Tie the rope carefully round the body and under the arms and the other end to the truck, then tow him across the border and leave him there. Whatever you do, make sure the Russians don't see you."

"Hang on Doug, I can't do that, I'll never be able to get him across on the main road, they have got a manned barrier there."

"Right, well done, turn off the main road and take a side turning. Now get the keys to the garage,

170

you know where they hang, and you only need the keys to the truck, they are... here in my pocket."

There was loud laughter coming over the phone now, and then there was a pause, before he said, "Forget it Ken, we are having you on, we are having a good time here, sorry you can't be with us, have a drink, but keep sober in case we have a real incident."

I took Quicky with me, wherever I could, and she was usually waiting patiently in the car, but of course on some of the investigations, she could not come along.

Early in 1947, Quicky had got out of the garden at Rüstern Allee and was roaming around somewhere, which she had done before, having always returned, but she had not got back when I had to leave on a complicated case, which lasted all day. When I got back and asked one of the sergeants where Quicky was, he said, "I don't know Ken, I haven't seen her, but Dougie wants to see you."

I ran up the wide staircase, taking two steps at a time, and went into his office, "Ah, Ken, you are back at last, take a seat." Then he looked long at me, sighted and said, "Sorry Ken, I have bad news for you. Somebody brought Quicky back in a jeep. She has been killed in an accident."

"Oh, my God, where is she, I must see her."

"Sorry, you can't. She was so badly injured that we did not want you to see her. We had a box made for her by the carpenter and buried her right in the back of the garden. He also made a plaque for her, with her full name and today's date. It looks very nice and the gardener has put some flowers on her grave. Come on, I show you where it is."

Dougie took me to the end of the garden and showed me the beautiful grave near the rear exit, into the road at the back of our building. I could not help but shed a few tears at the loss of my faithful dog and the kind actions of all my friends.

I did not know then, that one day I would go to Berlin with my wife Joyce, and walk along the Rüstern Allee to show her the villa I had worked in over fifty years ago. On an impulse I rang the bell and told the occupant that I had been stationed in his house at the end of the war and that I had just been showing it to my wife.

"Come on in and bring your wife in. Funny you should call, some time ago an Englishman came in and said he had been stationed here with the Military Police and we showed him round." He offered us some tea and showed us round the house, which had not changed very much, in all these years. I badly wanted to see if Quicky's grave was still there and told him the story, "Oh, so sorry, I will take you into the garden, but we have sold off the end of the garden some years ago and they have built a house on the ground." He took us down the garden and I looked at the house at the back, knowing that somewhere under there was my dog Quicky.

One day soon after this episode Dougie called me into his office and said, "We have a highly confidential case here referred to us from London, involving a British officer stationed here in Berlin. I will need you to help me with interviewing some

German civilians, who are also deeply involved. Under no circumstances must you discuss this with anyone here. I shall be working on the case with a Col. Donaldson, who is a CID officer, and who will be joining us from London shortly."

The case became later known as Operation Bernhard. The Bank of England had sent a request to us in Berlin to investigate the claim of a Capt. H., who had handed a badly burned metal cash box, containing hundreds of large white, singed, barely recognisable, five-pound notes, to a London bank. He asked for them to be exchanged, claiming that the metal safety cash box had been in a house that been bombed, and that he had only been able to recover the box recently. As the five-pound notes had been compressed, they stuck together and could not be easily separated. Capt. H. was told that the notes would have to be examined and checked, and that he would be notified as soon as the branch was given the OK by their head office. He left the address of the unit he was stationed with in Berlin.

The Bank of England forwarded to us the metal cash box containing this large amount of five-pound notes, with a comprehensive covering report whichwent, briefly telling us: -

> The cash box and the notes given to us by Capt. H were examined in our scientific laboratory, who came up with the following conclusions: -

> Five-pound notes are printed on specially selected paper, on one side only, with a large watermark. This watermark was more

pronounced than on genuine British notes and it was established that the notes supplied were forgeries. They had been printed in the Sachsenhausen concentration camp and had not been damaged by fire in the badly burned cash box at all, because prior to being burned, they would have been too large to fit into the cash box. The notes had actually been burned, stacked up, with the fire being carefully controlled, so that they would not be destroyed, but could be seen to be British five-pound notes. Burning the notes causes them to shrink and they only fitted into the cash box after shrinking.

Himmler had ordered the printing of these forgeries in 1942, with the object of flooding the international market, attacking the integrity of the Bank of England and causing financial embarrassment to Britain and its Allies. His scheme went under the secret code of 'Operation Bernhard'.

When Capt. H. was interviewed, he confessed that neither the cash box nor the money was his. He had been approached by a concentration camp survivor, who told him that he had hidden the cashbox containing the five-pound notes in the cellar of his house before the war. After he was freed from the camp he returned home to Berlin, to find his house had been bombed out and was a complete ruin. He dug into the cellar and managed to recover the badly burned cash box, with the money still inside. As he had no means of travelling to England or changing the English currency in Germany, he asked Capt. H. to take the box with him to London, when he next went on leave, and change the currency for him. Capt. H. felt sorry for the ex-prisoner, who had not only lost his home, but also all his family during the war, he agreed to do this for him.

It came out clearly during the investigation that this ex-prisoner had actually worked on the printing presses during the war, taking quite a horde with him when he was liberated. Capt. H. was court-martialled for his offence, stripped off his rank and discharged.

We found out later that SS Col. Kruger was in charge of Operation Bernhard, reporting direct to Himmler. He had specially selected some thirty inmates to print the forgeries. Amongst them was writer and artist Peter Edel who worked on and engraved the printing plates. He survived the camp and published two books about this time in Germany *Wenn es ans Leben geht* (When your life is threatened). He died in Berlin in 1983.

SS Col. Kruger personally recruited a professional Polish crook, Saly Smolianoff, who was also a forger. The special paper used was supplied by a paper mill in Hanover called Hannah Müller, who had the job of matching the special British paper. The prisoners working on the forgeries were given special treatment and slightly better rations, and were moved with the presses into different camps. Most of them survived their time in the concentration camp. The Nazis dumped the printing presses in an Austrian lake just before the end of the war.

Life in Berlin was a false life. We lived like Lords, we were the Masters, we had won the war and we were the Victors. We could do as we pleased. Food and drink were cheap for us. But I knew it was a false life, that it had to end some time, that I would have to get demobbed, go back to London, find a job and start afresh.

I had also fallen in love with Hildegard and wanted to marry her. That was very difficult, as one had to apply for permission from the army to get married, which took about twelve months. As Hildegard was a Christian and I was Jewish, we could not get married in church, but I had to find an officer who was also a Registrar. When I eventually found one, I discovered that he was also Jewish. His first words were, "You ought to be castrated wanting to marry a Christian German. What about your family, how do they feel about it? Well, never mind, if that is what you want, I will marry you, when the papers come through."

One of the conditions before getting permission to marry was to go on leave to England for two weeks, to discuss this matter with your family. In the summer of 1947 I spent two weeks with my cousin Inge and her daughter Charlotte at their house in Maida Vale. I immediately felt at home, as it was so refreshing to be back in England, where life was normal and where I was free of the pressures in Berlin. We went out to the theatre and saw English plays and an opera at Sadlers Wells. I met up with my cousin Lawrence, who was 15 years older than me, but still had been in the army with me, in the 87th Company of the Pioneer Corps.

When I saw Lawrence he said to me, "I have just heard from Helene Weber, you probably don't know her, but she is still alive, has survived the war and now lives in Berlin. I have got her address here, please look her up and help her with anything you can, perhaps you can take her some coffee as a present from me?"

"No, I have never heard of her, and of course I can take the coffee, but is she related to us?"

"Well, in a way she is. She is a very nice and highly intelligent woman. Helene was a very close friend of your uncle, Max Würzburger and us. They had an illegitimate son, called Wolfgang, who is of course a cousin of yours, and was born sometime in 1924, quite a long time before Max was divorced from your aunt Clasine, Inge's mother. They had wanted to get married, but in the end Max never married her, left Frankfurt and went to live in Paris. Inge, who is also a cousin of Wolfgang's and I had always kept in close touch with her, even after Helene and Wolfgang moved to Berlin. When Inge and I moved to London and got divorced there, we still heard from her, but lost touch during the war. It was lovely to hear from her again, it was only a very short letter, and she never mentioned Wolfgang, try and find out what happened to him."

So this was another skeleton that had emerged from the family cupboard. I had never met my uncle Max, my father's brother, as he had left Frankfurt when I was still quite young, but I had known his wife, my aunt Clasine and saw her whenever I visited Lawrence and Inge, to play with their daughter Charlotte and to go swimming with her.

I had heard that when Max married Clasine, she came from a rich family and was given a very large dowry. He invested it immediately in a company manufacturing bricks, believing that there would be a lot of building in the prosperous pre-war Germany before WW1. Unfortunately he was quite wrong, the company went bust and they lost all their money. Clasine's family bailed them out and he did quite well again. He was called up, served in the German army during WW1 and settled down again after the war, losing again more money during the inflation, but recovering again after some time. Apparently this scenario kept repeating itself when he lived in France.

In the summer of 1937 I visited, together with my father, my brother Walter in France. Walter had managed to get a labour permit to work in a dance band in a small seaside resort called Quend Plage, just North of Abbeville, for the summer and had invited us to join him there during my school holidays. As Papa could only stay with us for two weeks, we took him to the nearest railway station, where we could put him on a through train to Frankfurt, to be picked up by Mama at the station.

I stayed on until the end of the holiday season, playing on the beach and enjoying the freedom of living in France as an equal and marvelling at the differences in some of the life styles, as for instance men's toilets, which did not have seats, but you had to crouch down.

Walter now took me along with him to Paris, as I still had a week of my school holiday left. He had a room there in a flat in Clichie, where he stayed most of the time when he was in Paris and the landlady made me very welcome there. He showed me all around Paris and wanted to take me to see our uncle Max. Unfortunately he was away on business and Walter said, "This means that he must be doing well at the moment. It's a pity that he is out of town, he would have loved to meet you. He is always up and down with his business. Sometimes he is very well off, and then the next moment he is flat broke and has nothing. Did you know Bubie, that he is an excellent chess player, as a matter of fact a master of some sort or other? When he is down on his uppers he goes to one of the cafes where they play chess, sitting out in the front on the boulevard. He sits down and joins in, wins and loses a few games and then suggests that they play for money. Again he wins one and loses two games, suggesting now that they should play for a much larger sum, so that he can get his money back. The guy usually thinks that Max is a right sucker, agrees to play, Max mates him in just a few moves, scoops up the winnings and shoots off."

I remembered all that when I was back in Berlin. As soon as I had some time off, I drove in a jeep to Helena Weber's address. Fortunately she was in, and when I told her that Lawrence had given me her name and address, she asked me to come in. When I gave her my old name and told her that I was the youngest son of Siegfried, she immediately embraced me and said in German, "You must be Bubie, I remember you when you were a very

179

young boy, but no doubt you don't remember me. I can see you are in the British army now, you must tell me all about yourself, and what about Siegfried, Trude and your brothers?"

We sat down and I told her all about us. She started crying when she heard that my parents and brother had been killed in the holocaust. She then made some coffee from the packet I had brought along from Lawrence, and we settled down to chat.

She told me that she had brought Wolfgang up on her own, with very little help from Max. She never told Wolfgang anything about his Jewish father nor did she enter Max's name on his birth certificate. When the Nazis came to power she took the calculated risk of keeping this fact secret, as under the Nazi regulations you had to prove that you were of pure Arian descent for three generations. Wolfgang would have been considered to be Half Jewish, and hiding the fact that you had Jewish blood in your veins was a criminal offence. By 1941 Half Jews were also sent to concentration camps and many perished in the holocaust. As Wolfgang was born in 1924, had gone to school, passed his Abitur ('A' Levels) at Easter in 1942, and as he was considered to be an Arian, he was immediately called up into the German army. After his training, he joined the infantry, to be sent to Russia where he was killed in action, and I now realised how easily I could have killed my own cousin, had he been posted to the Western front, instead of the Russian front.

Since August 1944, Helene had been hiding a German officer, who had been involved in the 20th July plot to assassinate Hitler, in her house in

Berlin. The Gestapo arrested them both at the end of March 1945. Fortunately the Russians entered Berlin and liberated them before they could be executed.

Before returning to Berlin I bought 1000 cigarettes, as they were used as hard currency on the black market, and the largest salami I could get hold of for Hilde and her family. As I walked across the courtyard of the house in Ranke Strasse, Quicky recognised my footsteps and barked like mad, Hilde let her out and she ran down the three flights, leaping up at me, jumping into my arms.

Eventually in October 1947 all the necessary papers came through and our wedding was arranged to take place in the offices in Rüstern Allee. The whole SIB section took three days off, the APM and the Provost Marshall joined in the three-day party and we all had great fun. Fitz's wife insisted on taking all the photographs and in the end I was told that the films had been spoilt. I suspect that this was deliberate, as they hated the Germans and did not approve of my marriage.

After the three day military party, we had a private reception at Hildegard's mother's flat for all her family. Her estranged father Adolf came to this party as by this time we had become great friends.

Adolf left his wife Elsbeth and the two children Heinz and Hildegard in the mid 1920s. He was a high-ranking Communist official in the German Communist party, travelled a lot and met a French girl in Paris, called Emily sharing his views, who he later married. He was dispatched to Moscow, where he met Molotov and spent some time with

Emily in a Russian Communist holiday home at the Black Sea. Elsbeth took on a job as a porter in a large block of flats in the Ranke Strasse, near the Gedächtnis Kirche, bringing up the children on her own. She managed to send Heinz to a grammar school, but could not afford to do the same for Hildegard, but managed to get her an apprenticeship in a hairdressing salon.

When Hitler came to power in January 1933 Adolf fled to Czechoslovakia, crossing the border at intervals distributing anti-Nazi leaflets in Germany. His wife Emily stayed in their flat in Berlin. On one such sortie in March 1933 he was caught, arrested and sent for trial. He was very fortunate to be given a 10-year prison sentence. Had he been caught at a later date, he would not have had a trial, but would have been sent straight to a concentration camp. Now he was safe in prison

In late 1942 he was a prisoner in Alexander Platz Prison in Berlin, when it was bombed. The outside wall of the prison collapsed, he walked out and went to the basement flat of his wife. He stayed with her for a few days, but as he had no papers or ration cards, he decided that he should report back to the police. On arrival back at the prison they were surprised to see him, as they thought he had been killed. He was promptly locked up again and when his prison sentence finished, he was handed over to the Gestapo. Unfortunately for him he was sent to the concentration camp at Oranienburg. He survived as a political prisoner and was released from Oranienburg when the Russians liberated the camp. He went back to Berlin. Hildegard met him shortly after we had become friends and told him that she had a British soldier friend, who spoke fluent German and invited him to meet me.

His reply was short and curt. I am not going to sit down at the same table with a British capitalist.

Well spoken, but me a British capitalist? I got very intrigued and wanted to meet this man of spirit and principle and asked Hildegard to work on him, to see if she could change his mind.

We finally managed to meet and the more we got to know each other, the better we got on. That is how I got to know his full and interesting story.

Adolf became very disillusioned with the German Communist party and the Russian regime in Berlin. All the other communist survivors got themselves important jobs in post war Berlin, taking over some of the splendid Nazi villas, which had not been bombed out. Adolf was offered the post of Senior Parks Director of the county of Brandenburg, with a large villa to go with it

I asked him why he didn't accept the job and the house to go with it.

He looked me straight in the eye and said, "I told them I am not a Parks Director. I am a park attendant. I am a worker. I am a communist. I want my job back as a park keeper and I want to live in the basement flat with my French wife, that is where I belong."

I admired his fortitude and spirit. He did not take advantage of the fact that he had suffered persecution, prison, and had been in a concentration camp all because of the Nazis.

Unfortunately Emily died of tuberculosis on the 21st January 1947. He stayed on in his basement flat and died of influenza 11 months later, on the 16th December 1947, shortly after I had left Berlin for England to be demobbed. Hildegard had to travel separately to England two weeks later as a war bride. Maybe Adolf would not have caught influenza and his wife might not have died, had he accepted the offer of the job with the house, and not returned to his damp, cold basement flat.

I also believe that he died of a broken heart, because all his life he had fought for communism, the dictatorship of the proletariat, for the equality of the working classes. The reality that came with it was nothing that he had ever envisaged. He must have wondered what he had fought for.

In my mind I can still see him riding his little two-stroke motorbike in Berlin. He looked such a lonely figure riding off into the distance, which was the last time I saw him, before returning to England.

Demobbed

On the 10th December 1947 I arrived too early at the Charlottenburg railway station to leave Berlin for the last time on the military night train to Hannover. The Transport RSM immediately pounced upon me, "Excellent, you are off to Hannover? Well you will be in charge of the guard. What is your name?"

"Hang on Sergeant major, I am off to be demobbed at the Hannover demobbing centre, I am finished with all this, surely you can find someone else?"

"You are not demobbed yet mate, and you won't be until you get to Blighty, so guard commander you are going to be, like it or not. Put your name, rank and number on this form, sign it now and give it back to me. Tear off the copy, take it with you and hand it to the Transport Officer in charge at Hannover station. A corporal and five men have been allocated to you, their names are on this form, which you will also have to hand in, together with the rifles and ammo, when you arrive in Hannover. You can then discharge the guard and report to the demob centre, which is not far from the station. The Transport Officer (T.O.) can lay on transport for you. I see you have got your pistol on your belt, so you are OK. Here are the instructions for the guard, who are here already in their coach and have been issued with their equipment. Make sure you patrol the train regularly as laid down. Don't mess with the Russky's if they stop the train on route, but accompany them, when they get on to inspect the train, making sure none of our soldiers get off. Shortly before the train leaves at 10pm, patrol the train and see to it that no German fräuleins have sneaked on and that all the doors are locked before the train leaves. Keep a good look out of the windows until the train crosses into the Russian zone, watching out that no one jumps it to get out of Berlin. Good luck Staff."

He snatched the form I had completed and signed out of my hand, smiled, smartly about turned and marched off to his duty hut.

Paddy and Dougie, who had brought me to the station laughed out loud and helped me take my kit to the coach. As I had to sort out the guard, I did not have time for a last drink with them as planned, but said my farewells. It was just my bad luck to get lumbered.

I found the boys in the second coach where they had reserved three compartments. I bagged one of them, put my kit in, made myself comfortable and then called them in to give them their orders. Two men to be on guard for two hours at a time, and four men to be off guard. I told the corporal and the men that I would check the passengers before we left, that the corporal and I would lock the train doors before departure, giving the corporal one of the keys I had been given. I gave them all strict instructions that if the train was stopped during the night at one of the stations, and any Russian officers wanted to get on to inspect the train, to call me immediately. I sent the two who were on duty first, patrolling up and down the train telling them to make sure that there were no passengers without warrants on the train and to report back to me.

I called the corporal in saying, "I am going home to be demobbed and I know you are going on leave. Now we don't want the Russky's to hold the train up. So we just have got to make sure that none of the boys has smuggled a German girlfriend aboard to get her out of Berlin. I have got a bottle of Scotch with me, and if any Russian officers come aboard, we take them to this compartment, have a drink with them and hopefully one of them speaks German, then we can communicate with them, because I am bilingual."

"That's great," he replied. "I have a few cans of beer in my compartment and will gladly join in for a drink to speed up any train inspection."

At 21.45 the gate to the platform was closed. I called the corporal and the two men on duty and we walked along the train. It was quite crowded and everybody was in high spirits, as most of them were going home on leave. On our way back, the corporal and I locked all the train doors, whilst the two guards leaned well out of the windows to finally make sure that no one else was trying to get on the train. Punctually at 10pm the steam engine hooted loud and with a lot of jerks the train started slowly to get into motion. I leant out of the window of my compartment, reminiscing, having a last look at Berlin, the town I had got to like so much and in which I had spent nearly three years of my life. I had lived there like a prince, taking advantage of all the benefits a British soldier enjoyed in this conquered city, having unlimited access to English cigarettes, which were like gold dust.

I was fully aware that I had enjoyed many additional benefits, having been attached to the 89 SIB section of the Military Police, giving me many privileges. I had been quartered in a beautiful villa in Charlottenburg, in my own room. We had a well stocked bar in the huge wood panelled dining room with a big staff of Germans waiting on us and German secretaries, who typed all our reports. At the slightest excuse we threw all-night parties with whisky, three star Hennessey, Benedictine and other liqueurs flowing freely. The cost of these drinks was infinitesimally small for us. I knew that this life style was now finished for me, that it had not been real. I would have to start afresh, when I came home to Blighty. As we slowly left the town and its suburbs and entered the forests surrounding the city, I wondered whether I would ever see Berlin again.

I closed the window and settled down comfortably for the night, when I was woken up by the engine hooting loudly, the buffers of the coaches noisily hitting each other, as the engine driver applied his brakes and the train came to a shuddering halt. I looked at my watch; it was 2.30 in the morning. I opened the window; saw that we had pulled up at a station and that a group of heavily armed Russian soldiers stood on the platform.

This was the last thing I wanted to happen. I got the corporal out of the next compartment, went to the door at the end of the coach and opened the window. A Russian officer stood outside and said, "Inspektione."

I unlocked the door, opened it and the Russian officer came up the steps, accompanied by an ordinary soldier. I addressed him, "Tovaritch, Sprechen Sie Deutsch?" (Comrade, do you speak German?)

"Ja, ich spreche etwas Deutsch," replied the soldier in very good German.

I now knew the drill from my experiences with the Russian Military Police in Berlin. I gestured to them to follow me and the corporal, leaving one of the guards at the door, telling him not to let any more Russians on board, but if one of them became insistent, to bring him to me. I asked the two Russians to take a seat in my compartment, sat down opposite them, smiled and said in German, "I am SQMS Kenneth Ward and I am in charge of this train. I am stationed in Berlin as a member of the British Military Police and have been there for the last three years. I work very closely together with my friends in the Russian Kommandantura in Berlin. Most of the soldiers on this train are going to England on leave. I have personally checked all the papers of everyone on board and there are no Germans on this train. As we have to change trains in Hannover for a train going to Calais, which only runs once a day and is due to leave within an hour or so of our arrival, I would be very grateful if you would not delay us too much for your inspection. However, we still have time for a quick drink. Unfortunately I cannot offer you some of your excellent Vodka, but I have a very nice bottle of Scotch whisky right here in my bag, which I am sure you will like."

Having made my introductory speech, pretending that I was also going on leave, I pulled out a bottle of Scotch and poured a generous shot each into four mugs. Their eyes lit up and I had noticed that the Russian soldier had understood every word I had said. As expected, he had not bothered to translate into Russian to his officer, except for a few words when I had mentioned that this was a leave train. This confirmed my suspicion that he was a political Commissar, wore as usual no insignia, but was obviously in charge.

As we toasted each others health I remarked, "On my return to Berlin from leave, I will tell my friend at the Kommandantura, that I have met you both here at this station and how co-operative you have been," raising my mug for another toast.

The Russian soldier smiled and said, "I know what it is like to go home on leave, journeys always take too long and you can never get home quick enough. I tell you what I will do for you, I accept what you have said, there will therefore be no need for us to walk right through the train to inspect papers. Let's have another drink, your Scotch is perfect and kinder to the tongue than vodka, and then we will leave the train. I will phone through along the line ahead to the other stations, telling them that this is an English leave train, and that it must not be stopped."

He raised his mug, emptied it in one gulp and held it out for a refill. They drunk up quickly and raised to get out. I looked at the bottle, which was still half full. On an impulse I offered the bottle to the two Russians saying, "Many, many thanks, unfortunately we haven't got enough time to finish the bottle between us, take it with you and drink to us. I will always remember how kind and helpful you have been and mention it in the right places. Take care and good luck."

They went to the door of the coach, descended and I firmly locked the door, leaning out of the window waving to them, as the train slowly puffed and huffed, sounded its whistle, pulling slowly out of the station, with me feeling very relieved.

The Russian had kept his word; we accelerated through the night and arrived at Hannover an hour earlier than scheduled. The Transport Officer at the station was surprised when we checked in with our equipment and papers. Apparently it had been the fastest journey of the British train from Berlin through the Russian Zone since the service had started. I dismissed the guards, put my kit into a jeep supplied by the T.O. and set off to report to the demob centre.

Disillusionment set in on arrival. We came to a huge old German military barracks, which had been taken over by the army, drove alongside the huge parade ground, on which an RSM was drilling a squad of soldiers, who were running up and down at the double. You could hear his booming, barking voice miles away. We pulled up outside a side building and the driver helped me take my kitbag in, leaving me at the reception desk. I reported to the orderly officer, telling him that I was on demob leave and handed him my papers.

He said, "Staff, it will take me some time to prepare all the necessary documents, you must be tired after that slow, long boring train journey from Berlin. The Sergeants quarters are up on the first floor, you are in room 4. Make yourself comfortable, The Sergeants mess is on the ground floor, you won't be expected to do any duties here, but as this is now also a training regiment, we expect you to turn out smartly, with all your equipment blancoed and brightly polished. You will not walk across the parade ground but walk smartly around it, to set the rookies an example. I will book you onto a train to Calais for 10 am tomorrow. Come and see me this afternoon at 4pm, and I will then give you all further details."

What a come down from my privileged position in Berlin. I lugged all my kit upstairs, found room 4, which had a bed on each side with a spacious wardrobe at the foot ends. There was a table and some chairs in the centre of the room and two easy chairs by the window, overlooking the parade ground. In one corner was a hand washbasin with running hot and cold water and a mirror above it. This was the total of all the bare amenities. One bed was obviously occupied, with some equipment lying on it. I bagged the other bed, put some of my stuff in the wardrobe, shut the window to kill the noise coming from the parade ground, closed the curtain, stripped off and went to bed for a snooze. It was still only 10am and I could sleep for three hours, as lunch would not be before 1pm. I dozed off very quickly, the long journey and the drink had taken their toll.

Sergeant Bullen of the 8th Hussars walked in and woke me up. He was going back to his unit in Berlin and was waiting to catch the night train. He said, "I missed the train last night because the f......g duty officer decided to put me in charge of the guard last night, as though they haven't got enough NCOs of their own. You are lucky they didn't put you on guard tonight. Keep your head down and let's go for lunch. It's not a bad Sergeants mess, but I am sure you have eaten better. At least it is not as bad as the compo boxes we had to put up with when we were in action. By the way, there is a shower room right next door. Come on, let's go."

The rest of the day went on uneventfully. I reported to the orderly officer at 4 pm and he had all my papers ready for me:

"Right Staff, have a good journey home. The train leaves at 10am sharp from the main station and there will be transport for you at the main gate at 9.30am. As the train to Calais takes twelve hours, book some sandwiches for the journey in the mess tonight and tell them you want them ready for collection at breakfast. You lucky bugger, I wish I was going home tomorrow. Good luck in Civvy Street."

I managed to get a window seat on the train and did not feel like chatting much to the other sergeants who were making themselves comfortable. The train journey was slow and I was watching the passing countryside through the billowing smoke, coming from the ancient steam engine, puffing exhaustedly in front of our coach, whenever we went up a slight incline. I looked at the mountains, forests and rivers as we steamed along slowly. The towns and villages still showed the effect of war with houses, churches and farms in ruins. When we passed through small villages, I could see the drab-looking inhabitants standing at the barriers, looking forlornly at us, passing in our luxurious train. When we stopped at major stations, there were still the advertising hoardings on the platforms, with hand written notes and photographs of German soldiers, who had not yet returned from the war, with the relatives asking, "Do you know Hans Schmidt, Feldwebel (Staff Sergeant) in the 49th Infantry regiment, last heard of at Stalingrad?"

It was so pitiful, that two and half years after the war finished, hundreds of thousands of German soldiers were still missing and would not be heard of for a long time, even if they had survived, but had been taken prisoner by the Russians. The Germans were still suffering very badly from the after-effects of the war they had started and were feeling very sorry for themselves. I was glad I was getting out of it all.

We were late in arriving and were quartered in barracks near the station, as the ferry would not leave until the morning. We rose early, had a real English breakfast, which I had not had for a long time and made our way to the quay. We did not have to wait long, before we were allowed to board the ferry. It was 10 am by now. I found a nice deck chair below deck, as it was still quite chilly, and made myself comfortable.

After we had travelled for an hour or so, I made my way to the bow of the ship, as I wanted to watch as we entered Dover harbour. I remembered how I had first come to England in August 1939 seeing the British coastline for the first time in my life. I now saw ahead of me, in the far distance, the White Cliffs of Dover. I had the same feeling as then, with tears welling up in my eyes, when I still remembered as I had felt then, as free as the seagulls, noisily flying round the ferry. Yes, I was free again, free from the army, free and far away from Germany and the Germans, who had killed my parents and my brother, and who had taken my school life and my home away from me… and then the music stopped playing.

I was now coming again to the country of my choice, which had saved my life, had made me so welcome many years ago. Yes, I was coming back to my new home. I would have to start a new life, find a job and accommodation. I was prepared for all that, as we steamed slowly into the harbour. At last I was home again.

EPILOGUE

After Ken was demobbed, he set up home in England with Hildegard. It was very difficult for them to find rented accommodation, as many landlords were not willing to accept them so shortly after the end of the war, Hildegard being a German who had lived in Nazi Germany throughout the war and Ken being Jewish. They managed to find a furnished flat in Golders Green, in London, where they had to live frugally, as it was very difficult for Ken to find a job. The returning war veteran was very disappointed when he was told at the labour exchange, that the only training course they could offer was to go down the welsh coalmines. When he refused, his records were marked: - 'No suitable job could be found for this man'

By recommendation he found work with an Optical Company, working first in the office and then selling spectacle frames as a travelling salesman to opticians. Although it was a very competitive market, he managed to sell into it very successfully.

After four years of scrimping and saving, they bought a house in Kilburn, and Kens brother Walter, who he had not seen since he had visited him in France in 1936, came over from Australia in early 1952, and stayed with them for about a year.

Hildegard took a lover, some time before their son Stephen was born in October 1952, but in spite of this, they decided to continue to stay together. As life at home became more difficult Ken also took a lover in 1956.

Also in October 1952, Ken managed to change work and joined Scholl U.K Ltd, working his way up from shop manager to Research & Development and Quality Assurance manager, his work causing him to travel frequently abroad on business. He was responsible for developing many new Foot Care products, including the famous Scholl Wooden Exercise Sandals. They moved out of London in 1960 to Billericay in Essex, and from there in 1963 to Wickford, where they bought a bungalow, standing in one acre of ground, so that their son Stephen could keep his own pony.

Memorial wall in Frankfurt

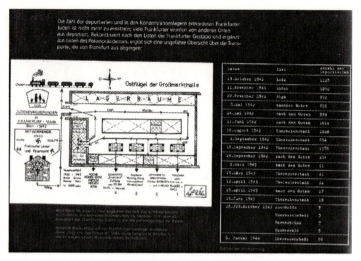

Plan of Deportation from Groß Markthalle

Both had given up their lovers but Hildegard became increasingly difficult and jealous of Ken's concentrated commitment to work. Life became intolerable and they separated in February 1968, after having been together for 20 years.

In May 1968 Ken and his newfound partner Joyce set up home together, married in 1971, and had two children Adam and Carla, moving to a more modern bungalow in Wickford. Ken progressed at work; extending his responsibilities further, to include Regulatory Affairs and Medical Research. When he retired in 1987, three different people took over his position.

Ken became a full time Technical Consultant, working for the company from home. This enabled him to see, and be involved in his children's upbringing. Ken was now attending international conferences, setting up European Standards for Medical Devices. Ken was retained when the company was eventually taken over by SSL

Ken with his family

International plc. and is still currently working for them.

In 1997 he was invited to visit his hometown by the city of Frankfurt, where he met the teachers from the Wöhlerschule, who asked him to give a talk to the students about his time at the school, during the Nazi persecution. Ken also visited the Memorial wall, erected by the town in the memory of the 11,134 Jews, deported in October 1941 and who all perished at Lodz. He was able to place stones on the protruding memory plaques embedded in the wall, which is a Jewish custom for gravestones.

On the 4th May 2001 he visited the Wöhlerschule again with Joyce, Adam and Carla, to be present at the opening of a Memorial Garden in the school grounds to all the Jewish pupils, who had not survived the Nazi regime, and at which the school orchestra played one of his father's compositions.

Living with Joyce and his two children he found himself, once again, in a close, happy, carefree and contented family circle, finally having found the same true happiness he had experienced during the first ten years of his life.

You will be able to read the full interesting story of Ken's life, so briefly described here, in his next book, to be published by Braiswick, so look out for it at www.braiswick.com

ABBREVIATIONS

A.P. Armoured piercing shell

ARM Assistant Provost Marshall

B.D..M. Bund Deutscher Madchen {Association of German Girls)

H.E. High explosive shell

H.J. Hitler Jugend (Hitler Youth)

H.Q. Head Quarters

L.S.T. Landing Ship Tank

Mensch German for 'Human' used colloquially for `great chap'

M. O. Medical Officer

N.S.D.A.P. National Sozialistische Arbeiter Partei (Nazi Party)

P.M. Provost Marshall

P.o.W Prisoner of War

P. U. Public Utility Vehicle R. B. Rifle Brigade

Red Caps Military Policemen

R.H.Q. Regimental Head Quarters

SHUFTY To have a look - Expression used bv members of the 8" army in the desert.

SIB Special Investigation Branch

S.Q.M.S. Squadron Quarter Master Sergeant

T.O. Transport Officer

Printed in the United Kingdom
by Lightning Source UK Ltd.
126302UK00001B/54/A